ORI DEVIR

OFF THE BEATEN TRACK IN
ISRAEL

Following the Israeli TV Series
NEKUDAT CHEN

ORI DEVIR

OFF THE BEATEN TRACK IN

ISRAEL

A GUIDE TO BEAUTIFUL PLACES

ADAMA BOOKS
NEW YORK

Ori Devir
OFF THE BEATEN TRACK IN ISRAEL

From the series **NEKUDAT CHEN**

Maps: Gaul Machlis
Translation from the Hebrew: Hazel Arieli
Photographs:
All the photographs in the book are by the
author except for the following:
Palphot: 17, 21, 31, 41, 49, 57, 73, 75, 77,
83, 85, 87, 91, 143, 147, 149, 151.
Dr. Uzi Paz: 23, 37, 45, 53, 55, 81, 135,
145, 178, 183.
Baruch Gian: 28, 79, 137, 139, 141.
Yaakov Shorer: 97, 101.
Elan Zaharoni: 93.

**Library of Congress Cataloging-in-
Publication Data**
Devir, Ori
  Off the beaten track in Israel.
  Translation of: Nekudat Chen.
  1. Israel — Description and travel —
  Guide-books.
  I. Title.
DS103.D9313 1985 915.694'0454 85-18603
ISBN 0-915361-28-0

Adama Books, 306 West 38 Street, New
York, New York 10018

Printed in Israel

There are always people who claim that
no matter what, they need one more
hour to finish a day's outing. This is
how we feel about completing this book
— except perhaps instead of hours, we
could use weeks. For their efforts in the
Hebrew edition, for their willingness
and above all their actual work, thanks
are due to the following: my wife
CHAVA, who commented on, read,
and typed part of the material, before
and after a day's work; SHULAMIT
LANGHOLTZ, the editor, who
grappled with the original manuscript;
GAUL MACHLIS, who produced the
maps; SHLOMO NAKAR; and
HAZEL ARIELI who translated the
manuscript; and to all the others who
each contributed in his own field.

My graditude is also due to the
photographers who contributed their
work: to the Survey of Israel, which
gave us permission to use the maps
which appear at the beginnings of each
section; and to those who helped
formulate the idea for the book and
implement it: the hikers, including my
family, my students, the people of the
TV show Nekudat Chen which inspired
this series: the producer, the editors and
the field crew. To be dragged over hills
and water, to crawl in caves and to
climb down mountains on rope is no
trifling matter, particularly with full
photographic equipment, and recording
and lighting apparatus. For long lovely
days, my thanks to all of them.

ORI DEVIR

CONTENTS

INTRODUCTION

It wasn't easy for us to select a few dozen sites from hundreds of truly beautiful places. Some of the better known spots had to be left out, and we also decided that this time, we would have to do without the cities.

We did include water sites, hills, desert, seashore and plain, a few sites near the road and some that can only be reached on foot. Even so, we couldn't resist the temptation and added a few famous places, such as Caesaria and Panyas.

We chose some sites near cities, so that people can discover what's "right under their noses" — for example, Miqwé Isr'el near Tel Aviv, or the Carmel sites near Haifa. Some monuments are also mentioned, even though they are not exactly beautiful sites. Thus, the Golani look-out post or the Negev Monument near Be'er Sheva found their way into the book.

Sometimes, a site has been included as a kind of clue to travelling a different way and visiting a new place; for example, a suggestion to travel between the North and the centre of the country via Samaria. These routes are not always shorter, but they are generally more beautiful.

Although this is a book about sites, we decided to include flowers here and there. How could we otherwise? But to tell the full story of the flowers of Israel would be a topic for another book.

Generally, the sites are presented in groups, for instance Nahal Kelah, Newé Yam, and the Carmel Caves; or the sites of Yeroham, Sede Boqer, the springs of Nahal Zin and Avedat. Even though this album is for armchair travellers as well as active explorers, I couldn't fight the tour-guide in me, and so I arranged the book accordingly: sites near each other are taken together, with maps at the beginning of each page, and instructions for getting to the various locations are included.

Finally, many important sites had to be omitted, and must await other books in the series.

Ori Devir

MAPS, ORIENTATION, NAMES, TRIPS, ETC.

The book is divided into seven sections, comprising almost the entire country. Each section has a short introduction and a map.

If looking at the photographs gives you an appetite to travel — please do. Here are some practical guidelines:

ORIENTATION ON THE ROADS

In the last few years road orientation has become easier than in the past. As in other enlightened countries, our roads have been numbered and kilometer signs have been set up. No longer do we have to say, "Take the Ramat Raziel Road." It's sufficient to give the number of the road and say simply: "Take Road 395". There is method to the numbering: the number of digits indicates the importance of the road and the kilometer numbers are in a consistent direction. The road numbers appear on signs on the road and on new maps, which also show the distances between junctions and important points.

MAPS

If you want to travel, it's worthwhile getting a good map.

MAP OF ISRAEL

Scale 1:400,000, published by the Survey of Israel. This is a small map, which is its advantage. Its disadvantage is that not all the details appear on it.

ISRAEL — TRAVELLING AND TOURING MAP

Scale 1:250,000, published by the Survey of Israel. This map is in two parts and more convenient.

MAPS FOR TOURING AND PATH MARKING.

Published by the Public Committee for Path Marking, scale 1:50,000, in Hebrew only. At several sites in Israel touring paths have been marked. In the field the paths are marked in color between two white stripes ▤ at reasonable distances from each other. On the maps the touring paths are marked in the same color and they include additional useful information. In our directions to sites reached by a marked path, we have indicated these in the description and by a symbol in the apprpriate color.

In some of the maps in the book the colors of the paths are marked in rectangles as they appear on the path marking maps. In places where two colors meet on the same path a line separates them ▤ - - - -▤ .

THE MAPS IN THIS BOOK

These are meant for general orientation. At the beginning of each section is a map that indicates sites in the book, which appear in a red triangle ▲, and other recommended sites in a blue triangle ▲. The three northern maps are based on the travelling and touring maps with a scale of 1:250,000; the other four are based on the map of Israel with a scale of 1:400,000. The scale is not uniform because the maps were reduced or enlarged as needed. At the end of roads the direction of travel is marked (pointing off the map) alongside the road. The small maps on each page are based on maps with a scale of 1:100,000. Some were reduced in being photographed and thus the scale is not the same for all. Notice the scale marked by lines at the edge of each map ⌞____⌟KM These maps also have an arrow pointing to the north and the numbers of the important roads. The directions for getting there are based on the road numbering and on the kilometer sign numbers. When the description gives the approach from a specific direction such as: "We come from Yeroham to Sede Boker," the kilometer number that appears first is the one we meet in the direction we are travelling, in this case between kilometers 133-132. If a specific direction isn't given, the numbers of the kilometer signs are in order of sequence, e.g. between kilometers 107-108.

Recently a new method of kilometer marking has been adopted in Israel. It is possible that in some places the old system will not yet have been changed. In such cases we have preceded the field workers and we hope it won't cause you to get lost. Unfortunately, the kilometer signs aren't always in place. Some have been shifted or sabotaged. The directions usually answer the question of how to get to a place. Sometimes there is also a suggestion for continuing the tour or for returning by another route. In the small maps on each page we have shown directions based on these larger maps. These are indicated by the marking.

PLACE NAMES AND SPELLING

To this day it is difficult to find uniformity in the spelling of place names in English and even in Hebrew there are many variations. For this reason there are also variations in the spelling of the English. It is possible that you will find one spelling in the text, another on the map and even a third on a road sign (e.g. Caesaria or Qesarya). We hope that at very least the sound of a name will be a sufficient clue. We have tried to give most of the names as they appear on the 1:100,000 scale map. Sometimes there are problems of transliteration from Hebrew into English. Some of the names are translated into English and are a little different from the usual spellings. For example, Nahal David is DAWID. Sometimes a name is spelled one way on the maps of Israel and another way on the road signs. We have tried to give both spellings, and as a result the spelling will not always be uniform.

The story of each site is given in a nutshell. Anyone who wants to expand his knowledge — to know more, to see more, to tour more, can refer to the literature on Israelography.

If it happens that the description of a route is not accurate, a path has become a road, a settlement has been added, or a site unearthed or a camping site opened, this is a sign that Israel is developing at a fast pace that is hard to keep up with.

GLOSSARY

In giving site names, we have used tranliterated Hebrew for most geographic information. A short glossary of these words follows — and this is a good opportunity for you to learn a new language . . .

Berekha	pool
Biq'a	valley
Emeq	valley
En (Ein)	spring
Gesher	bridge
Har	mountain
Horva	ruin
Mahtesh	crater
Mappal	waterfall
Ma'yan	spring
Me'ara	cave
Mehlaf	interchange
Mitzpe	observation post
Nahal	river, riverbed
Shemura	reserve
Tel	mound
Wadi	riverbed
Zomet	junction

LEGEND

	Pool
	Spring
	Mineral Spring
	Well
	Water hole
	Perennial stream and water fall
	Seasonal water course (wadi)
	Sand dunes
.200	Spot height (metres)
•200	Depth in metres
	Cliff
	Slope
	Wood or forest

	Railway and station
1	Motorway; Interchange
40	Main road
222	Regional road
	Other road
	Unmetalled road
	Dry-weather trac
15	Road distances in kilometres
	International boundary
	Cease-fire line, 1967
	Line of disengagement 1974
	Water canal
	Aqueduct
	Lake

	Built-up Area
HEFA	City, Population 150.000 or more
Akko	Town, Population less than 150.000
Nesher	Town, Population 10.000 or more
Dor	Town, Population less than 10.000
▪ Ilanot	Locality
∴ En Gedi	Ruin
Ψ	Ancient Synagogue
	Church or Monastrey
	Mosque
⊚ ○	Watertank, Water tower
•	Other tower
	Airport
	Airfield

ADDITIONAL CONVENTIONAL SIGNS ON PAGES 11.33.65

	Ruin
	Prehistoric site
	Restored historical site with indication of main period
	Other historical site
Ψ	Ancient synagogue
	Jewish place of pilgrimage or traditional tomb
	Important mosque
	Monastery, church or other Christian holy place
	Druze holy place
•	Bahai holy place
m	Museum or important collection-Archaeology or history
m	Natural science
m	Art and general
	Nature reserve
	Wood or forest, Oasis
	Field school

	Dual highway and bridge
	Main road, width 6.50 or more
	Main road, width less than 6.50 m
	Secondary road, width 6.50 m or more
	Secondary road, width 5.00 – 6.50 m
	Secondary road, width less than 5.00 m
	Picnic site
	Camping site
	Youth hostel
	Christian hospice
	Observation tower
	Observation point, Observation terrace
	Scenic point
▲	Other place of interest
	Mine or quarry
	Cave

	Colour-marked path and border between colours
4	Road numbers
▲	Site of Principal importance
▲	Site of Secondary importance
++++	Boundaries
	Road suitable for all vehicles and end of road
	Road for vehicles with four-wheel drive and end of road
	Foot path
	Site maintained by Nature Reserves Authority
	Site maintained by National Parks Authority
	Site maintained by Jewish National Fund

LEGEND ATTACHED TO SITE MAPS

	Motorway
	Main road
	Secondary road
	Railway
	Town
⊚	Settlement
	Perennial stream
	Seasonal watercourse (wadi)
•	Spring
	Ruin

MOUNT HERMON AND THE GOLAN

Today, Mount Hermon appears as the "Northern bulge" on the map. It is a large, high mountaineous ridge, and aside from being a kind of border-outpost separating Syria, Lebanon and Israel, it is also Israel's major source of water. Its melting snow supplies the springs of the Jordan river.

Mount Hermon and the neighbouring peaks, such as Har Dov to the West, are important observation points (they are referred to as the "eyes of the country"). It has many hiking paths and special scenic spots. However, because of its status as a lookout point, it is rarely used for hiking. Its snowy slopes provide skiing in the winter, and now, I hope, we will also learn to appreciate it in the summer. Its surroundings are very beautiful. The springs in the Hermon, Snir, and Dan Rivers provide scenic areas which are difficult to compete with.

Once, the Golan was regarded as a threatening region of fortifications manned by an enemy army . . . Today, travellers have come to know it well. We have found the ruins of ancient settlements there. There were once Jewish settlements here and these have provided us with the remnants of many synagogues. We have become acquainted with the volcanic hills and the special geological phenomena of the area, and we have learned that it is best to visit the Golan in the spring, the season when everything in the Golan is "in flux" — rivers, waterfalls, and vegatation. When we return in the summer, it is hard to believe that evrything which had been flowing and blossoming in the spring is now dry, and turned to black basalt —

Well, not quite everything.

The Gilbon River, Berekhat HaMeshushim, the Zavitan River, the Hermon River and other sites are a relief in the summer as well. If we'd like to walk in the snow — it's still possible. There is also the winter.

Skiing, Ice for Jerusalem, and Late Spring on
MOUNT HERMON

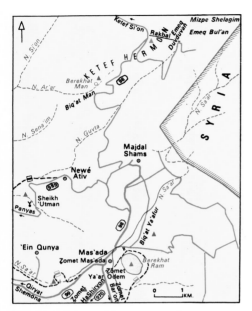

To get to Mount Hermon you have to go to the edge of the map and up to the northernmost corner. The first stage in the climb is the Druse village of Majdal Shams. If you are coming from the south drive along Road 98 or 978. If you are coming from Qiryat Shemona drive on Road 99 to Panyas; from Panyas you can reach the village by Road 989 via Newe Ativ or again by Road 98 from Mas'ada. If you are planning a winter trip, listen to the weather forecast before setting out, to make sure the road is open. And bring money (for entrance fees, cable car rides, equipment, etc.) and suitable clothes (sunglasses are very important). In summer it's a good idea to visit the Hermon on an organised tour.

▲
Skiing on Mount Hermon

Until the Six Day War, when the shoulder of the Hermon was captured by the Israeli Army, the snow-capped peak of "Grandfather Hermon" was remote and inaccessible. There were some daring individuals who ventured up the slopes, were caught and imprisoned — and released with a sackful of stories. But for most Israelis the Hermon was out of reach. The mountain mass — bigger and higher than anything in Israel's possession — was difficult to get to. A few villages with inconvenient approach roads did climb slightly up the mountain but they did not pass the 1,400 meter mark. Above this point there was typical high-altitude vegetation, then an area devoid of flora — and all blanketed in winter with snow.

In actuality, only a small part of the Hermon is in Israel's possession. The highest peak, the site of the ruins of an ancient temple, rises to an altitude of 2,814 meters. The highest peak in Israel's possession is Mizpe Shelagim, the "Snow Observatory," which stands at a height of 2,224 meters. Most vacationers spend their time near the upper cablecar station, which is much lower than the Snow Observatory. One need only remember that the Hermon is high, its streams feed the Jordan River, it looks out over a good part of Israel, it is a ski slope, it has Israel army outposts, and . . . it is an enchanting summer resort. We will come back to this point later.

The Hermon range has many names. The Bible mentions among others: Baal Hermon, Sirion, and Sion, and post-biblical literature refers to its Aramaic name, Toor Thalga. The Arabs call the Hermon Jabel A-Talg, which means the Snow Mountain, probably a carryover from the days when snow was brought from here to the ice boxes of Jerusalem. Today it is known in Arabic as Jabel A-Sheikh, Old Man Mountain — some say because of the white halo around its head.

Most of the Hermon has never been inhabited, but even so there are many stories connected with its slopes and ranges. Ancient dwelling sites and tools have been found here. We know of the Yitturs who lived in Chalkis, whose kingdom extended over part of the Hermon during biblical times. And there are references to a Jewish population that lived here in post-biblical times, as well.

Since the Six Day War, Har Hermon has changed. After roads were built by the Israeli Army, roads were also constructed on the Lebanese side. After the Yom Kippur War, during which the shoulder of the Hermon had fallen to the Syrians and was later recaptured, Israel set up additional outposts. Again, roads were constructed up and around the mountain. The Hermon, which until 1967 had been climbed by only a few, now became an area swarming with soldiers and . . . hikers.

Ski slopes, cablecars, toboggans, and dangerous nylon gliding sheets — that is the Hermon in winter. And in summer, the Hermon — unlike the rest of the country — is a riot of blossoms. The forested area ends quite low on the slopes and beyond Majdal Shams there are soon only solitary trees. But higher up there is flora chartacterized by patches of thistle (of which some 250 different varieties have been counted) and many, many flowers. Up here, spring comes late and lasts long.

Down below the hot, dry summer has arrived, while the visitor to the top can still enjoy the bloom of an extended and colorful spring. Remembering that the Hermon is a summer resort, too, perhaps makes us appreciate it even more.

▶ A kind of lotus on Mount Hermon

A Watchful Eye on the Hermon at
BEREKHAT RAM (Ram Pool)

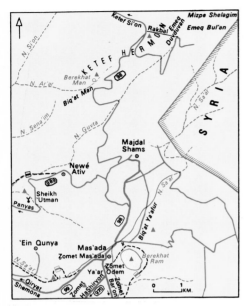

Take Road 99 from Panyas or Road 978 from the south of the Golan to the village of Mas'ada. From here it is a short way to the parking area and the look-out post at Berekhat Ram. But don't stop after you've seen the view from the look-out post; it's definitely worth taking a walk all the way around the pool or along the shore.

When Israelis rediscovered the pool after the Six Day War there were some who thought that Berekhat Ram was another of the many volcanic craters found in the Golan — one which had filled with water and formed a small lake. The ancients also had their hypotheses about the source of the water. Some said that the pool was part of a network of underground springs, dating from the time of Noah's Flood. Others did not enlighten us with information on where the water came from, but were able to tell us where it was going — in an underground channel to Panyas; and the Panyas Spring was simply the lower opening for the lake water. In order to back up this version, the pool was sometimes called "Lake Panyas." A "scientific" conclusion appears in Josephus Flavius' *The Jewish War:* "To all appearances the source of the Jordan is near Pamyas [*sic*], and indeed it springs from the pool known as the basin (Pialeh) and then flows below ground, and the pool is at the entrance to Trakhon . . . and because of its appearance the round pond is called a basin. And the water of the pool comes up to its mouth and never sinks lower nor overflows. Formerly nobody knew that the Jordan emerges from this pool, until Philippus, Prince of Trakhon, came and discovered it by an unmistakable sign: He sowed chaff in the basin and then found that the grains were carried to Pamyas, where the ancients had sought the source of the Jordan, and there it floated on the water." Apropos this little tale, there once was someone quite famous who wanted to use this channel to get into the country "through the back door." The story goes that when Moses learned that he would not be allowed to enter the Land of Israel, he attempted to get in through the channel of Caesarion, which is beneath the Panyas.

Our ideas about Berekhat Ram have changed since 1967. If we thought it was a few score meters deep, we were mistaken. It goes down no more than 8-10 meters. If we thought the water was unsuitable for swimming and that only frogs and such could dwell in it — we were wrong again: The water is good and has a low salt content.

Experts came, looked, tasted, and turned our basin "upside down." The pool is surrounded by basalt heaps and volcanic ash but also has ordinary sedimentary rock, a fact that upsets the theory of a "volcanic crater." But let's forget all this and consider the water. The water comes to the pool from the Hermon and it is in fact underground water that surfaces here. If it turns out that this underground water surfaces in the Panyas springs, then Philippus was right. Today, the pool serves as a reservoir from which water is pumped through pumping stations to the settlements in the northern Golan.

There are also some other theories we picked up from various guides:
1. The remains of an ancient temple stand on the peak of the Hermon. In the past, many pilgrims visited the site, walking great distances to do so. The dust from their long journeys stuck to their bodies and their clothes. As they wished to cleanse themselves before going up the holy mountain, they would scatter around the area to find their way to the springs. In doing so they would trample over fields and orchards, disturbing the farmers in their work. So what did the local people do? They got together and dug a large pond near the path up the mountain. As a result of generations of bathing pilgrims, the water became muddy near the edges.
2. Every winter thick layers of snow cool the Hermon's huge bulk. When spring comes and the snow melts, suddenly most of the mountain is exposed to the rays of the blazing sun. It gets really hot. In order to stay cool and fresh even on burning summer days, the Hermon bathes its feet in the basin of water . . .

▲
Threshing near Berekhat Ram

▶ Berekhat Ram on a rainy day.

Of Hashish, Mosquitoes, and a View at
MIVZAR NIMROD (Nimrod's Fortress)

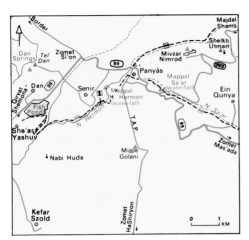

From Qiryat Shemona travel east on Road 99. A little beyond Panyas turn onto Road 989, which goes up towards Mivzar Nimrod, Nimrod's Fortress. Then turn left between kilometers 4-5. You can't miss it. When you get to know the landscape up there, with the fortress dominating the surroundings, you'll be able to make it out from almost any part of Galilee.

Before you begin your visit perhaps you should become acquainted with the fortress. The area was first inhabited by people of the Ismailiya sect, who became famous for, among other things, their methods of eliminating their enemies. They would drug some of their people with hashish, and then send them out on murder missions. In the course of time these people acquired the name Hashishin, which became bastardized in some European languages to "assassin." In the twelfth century, after being persecuted and slaughtered by their Muslim enemies, the members of the Ismailiya sect came to an agreement with the Crusaders. In exchange for shelter they gave the Crusaders Panyas and Kal'at-A-Subeibe.

The Crusaders at once set to work building and fortifying. At this stage, when Panyas and Kal'at-A-Subeibe became a bridgehead for the Crusaders to Damascus, the fortress began its "stormy life" and changed hands several times. At the end of the Crusader period, it was taken over by the Mamelukes, led by Babers. An inscription on one of the towers gives its date of construction as 1229. A large hall bears an inscription saying it was built in 1231. An inscription on a cistern mentions the date 1290. During the Mameluke period, Kal'at-A-Subeibe grew in importance and its governor was appointed directly by the Sultan of Cairo.

Various building styles and techniques, the result of the repairs and additions of all those who held the fortress, can be distinguished. On the way up to the site you will see a row of towers jutting out from the castle wall.

The fortress itself has several wings, each with a specific role: The citadel is on the top level, with the remainder below it. The fortress is over 400 meters long, and in certain parts its width reaches 100 meters.

The entrance to the fortress is through a breach in its western wall — the one next to the parking area. Near this opening, inside the fortress, is one of the cisterns designed to supply the needs of the residents both in times of peace and siege. A path between the ruins leads to the top of the tower; from here you will get a general view of the entire fortress. You can also visit the halls in the citadel, test the endurance of the gate towers, and see the many reservoirs. In the south-west tower there is a spiral staircase and if you find your way (careful, it's dark) and you are slim enough, you can slip out of the fortress through . . . a firing embrasure!

Finally — is there a connection between this site and the mosquitoes of the Hula Valley?

According to tradition, Nimrod, a descendant of Noah's and a great builder and hunter, had been charged by God to be lord of all creatures. When he went hunting all the animals and birds would fall to the ground before him. A thousand hills would produce food for him. And when he wanted to drink he would put his mouth to the Panyas, which would cast up its waves for him to imbibe . . . . In time, Nimrod's head was turned, and he said: I am the lord of all things. Who then is this God that I should sacrifice to Him? And Nimrod became insolent and shot threatening arrows skywards. But the One Sitting on High played a prank and returned Nimrod's arrows soaked in blood. And Nimrod boasted: I have defeated Him! But a heavenly voice was soon heard saying: Wicked one, I have a tiny creature down there in my world, a mosquito. Go and do battle with it! Nimrod went to fight the mosquito. The mosquito flew into Nimrod's nose, and from there it moved on to his brain where it buzzed and buzzed until finally he died. Kal'at-A-Subeibe, or Kal'at Namrod, is said to be his burial place. And this is the source of an additional name — Citadel of the Mosquitoes. To this very day mosquitoes rise from it in swarms and cover the entire area.

▲
Nimrod's Fortress — a view of the fortress and the citadel, which appears high up at the edge of the picture

▶ Nimrod's Fortress, a view from the Citadel

Three in One at
MAPPAL SA'AR (Sa'ar Waterfall)

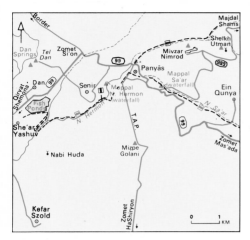

On Road 99, between kilometers 15-16 (nearer to 15), there is a small carpark (less than one kilometer from the Panyas site). Cross the road carefully and walk along the path to the waterfall observation post. This trip is recommended for winter, when the waterfall is active.

Nahal Sa'ar begins on the shoulder of the Hermon. From there it flows towards the Ya'afori Basin and then down the steep slope to join Nahal Hermon, which is the Panyas. The entire stream, from the Ya'afori Basin to its end, is about seven kilometers long, and on its way it descends about 500 meters. In fact, when you travel between Panyas and Mas'ada on Road 99, you are moving parallel to the stream. Here and there you can see it from the road, but at such a distance it's hard to make out what it is all about.

And what is it all about?

From winter through early summer, running water — water from springs and rains that once powered flour mills (one of which was in operation until only a few years ago). There are several waterfalls along the course of the stream as well as interesting geological phenomena. Altogether it is a pleasant trip.

Nahal Sa'ar also serves as a border marker, and this too is connected with a very interesting geological phenomenon. Whoever has travelled in the Golan knows that it is mostly basalt, which reaches up to the foot of the Hermon. Mount Hermon, on the other hand, is composed of limestone. And Nahal Sa'ar — have you guessed? Nahal Sa'ar passes between black and white — between basalt and limestone — and hops along between the two types of rock which form such different landscapes.

Another border can be seen at the stream near the Panyas site. The Crusader Fortress of Panyas stands to the south of the ponds, the spring, the carpark. Its southern wall stands next to Nahal Sa'ar, which serves as a southern border and a fortification. To stroll alongside the southern wall, to peek through the gate at the stream, and to walk along the path through the brush which grows on its bank — these are some of the most pleasant parts of a trip to the Panyas and the stream.

But . . . I almost forgot. The description of the approach leads us to the waterfalls near the road. The three Sa'ar Falls, known in Arabic as "Ga'dir El-Hamam," flow in winter and torrent in early spring. You can see them from the observation platform, or you can approach the fall itself. Careful!

If you see the waterfalls in full force at the beginning of spring, and then come back in summer when they are all dried up, you might very well think you have made a mistake and come to the wrong place.

▲
South Gate to the Crusader Panyas. From here there was a bridge over Nahal Sa'ar.

▶ The Sa'ar Waterfall

Panic at
CAESARIA PHILIPPI (Which Is Panyas)

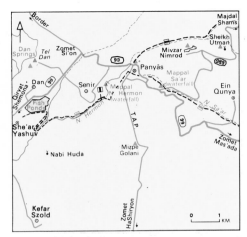

Travel east from Qiryat Shemona on Road 99 directly to Panyas. Betweeen kilometers 13-14 (just after 13) at Panyas there is a central parking area near the pools and the springs. That's it.

The historian Josephus wrote about a cave whose opening yawns above the pools: "And on the spur of the mountain below, there opens the mouth of a hidden cave, and near the cave what looks like a steep fissure in the rock, which sinks down to a deep chasm full of still waters. And people examining the depth of the water could not reach the bottom of the pond even with a very long rope. From the back of the cave leading outside the springs burst forth and this is the source of the Jordan according to some opinions . . . ."

The concluding words hint at the opinion that prevailed in Josephus' days — that this was the main source of the entire Jordan, thus the name, "the big Jordan" (the river descending from Tel Dan was accordingly called "the little Jordan"). Other people in other times have claimed that the source of the Jordan is in the beautiful pool known as Berekhat Ram, which has a channel connecting it to the Panyas.

Perhaps the solution to the origin of the name Panyas lies in the recesses of the caves in the cliff wall here. Long ago, a statue of the god Pan rested in one of the recesses. We know this from the Greek inscription carved here, which tells of a priest who dedicated a statue to the god Pan. In Greek mythology Pan, half man and half goat, with goat's hoofs and horns on his head, was the god of goatherds. He loved to play music, especially his reed pipe. When he wanted to gather his herd he played loudly and frightened the flock. Echo was a nymph who had lost her ability to speak and could only repeat last words or syllables spoken by others. The story goes that when Pan was disturbed in his sleep he would go wild and roll heavy stones down the cliffs, while Echo stood beside him repeating the cries of the frightened shepherds below . . . . *Pan*ic! In Arabic, which has no letter for the sound "p" the area is known as Banias. But this only confuses us in understanding its name.

To the west of the cave and its recesses, a bit higher on the cliff, is the grave of El-Hader. El-Hader is the Arabic name that generally refers to the Prophet Elijah and to Saint George. Panyas was sacred to several religions, including the Alawis, a semi-secret cult.

Not far from El-Hader, on the slopes, are the remains of a wall with diamond-shaped slabs. These might be the remains of a Herodian period structure which appears on the coins of Panyas-Caesarion as the emblem of the town during the time of Herod and his son Philippus.

Besides the water and the cave the Panyas contains the remains of a Crusader fortress whose wall borders the course of the Sa'ar River. There is also a flour mill, called Tachunat Matruf, and there are trees, running waters, and an "officers' pool" — a legacy from the Syrians, which Israelis now use.

And the Panyas also has a history. Around the year 200 B.C.E. (about 2,200 years ago) a battle was fought here between the heirs of Alexander the Great. As a result of this battle, the Land of Israel was won by the Salbeks (one of whose descendants was the evil Antiochus of the Chanuka story). Herod, the king who built so extensively all over the country, left his mark here as well. He built a large temple to the god Pan in honor of the Emperor Augustus and called the place Caesaria; and in order not to confuse it with the Caesaria on the Mediterranean shore he called this one Caesarion — the little Caesaria. It was also sometimes called Caesaria Philippi — after Philippus, one of Herod's sons. But at the end of the Second Temple period, under the rule of Agrippus II, the name was changed to Neronias, this time in honor of the Emperor Nero.

Moving on about a millenium to the Crusader period, Panyas became a border area between Moslim and Crusader factions and the town changed hands several times. After the Crusader period Panyas became less important, although the town with its fortress was still an important link on the road from Damascus to the sea.

▲
Statue niches at Panyas

▶ The Panyas pools and the grave of El-Hader

The Plane Tree that Parts
MAPPAL NAHAL HERMON (at Panyas)

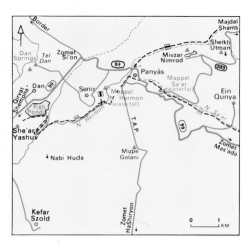

The best route? Go on foot from the "Officers' Pool" at the Panyas site along Nahal Hermon to the waterfall. A careful walk with pauses to look at the view should take about one hour. Or from Qiryat Shemona drive on Road 99 till it turns off to Snir between kilometers 12-13, and then follow the road signs to the parking area above the waterfall. From there go on foot.

Floating on inner tubes down Nahal Hermon. Don't try this without a guide.

For me personally, returning to the Panyas waterfall was like returning to a first love. And here is the true story. While I was still a boy in the youth movement, we toured the sources of the Jordan. One of our outings was to Panyas waterfall. Then, too, this waterfall was near the Syrian border and I do not remember if it was dangerous or whether our dear youth leaders simply turned the journey into an adventure. When we reached the spot, we stood near the cascading water with its flying droplets and vegetation and huge plane tree — and we felt as if we had conquered the whole world. Later there was the War of Independence, battles with the Syrians, and the fixing of the borders of the State of Israel. Above the Panyas waterfall there were Syrian outposts, and on the way to it a demilitarized zone and all kinds of other signs indicating one thing — Danger! Do not approach.

After the Six Day War I rushed to the waterfall, even before a path was cleared. I slid down the cliffs and blazed a trail. And the big waterfall? It was still there and seemed even more powerful. A white cloak of droplets on its sides and the plane tree in the middle stood stronger than ever.

Today the Panyas waterfall is a nature reserve and is actually in the Hermon River. But don't make the mistake of thinking that the waterfall is important only for the pleasant memories it brings. After all, it is one of the sources of the Jordan — Israel's main water supplier.

The Jordan has three main sources — the largest, which supplies almost half the Jordan's water, is the Dan. The other two, each of which supplies a quarter, are the Snir River (the Hatzbani) coming from Lebanon west of the Dan, and the Panyas, whose source is at the foot of the cliff on the Panyas site east of the Dan.

After World War I control of the Panyas began to shift between British and French spheres of influence. Its importance as a water source and its convenient northern pass at the foot of the Hermon, made it a strategic and financial asset. Finally a decision was made and the springs and the pass became French. Later they became Syrian. The waterfall is just beside the border. The Panyas — the Hermon River — continues on in a deep gorge. Then the landscape changes and the river flows at the edges of the Hula Basin until it joins the Dan north of Sede Nehemia. About here the party begins — both the Snir River and the Ayyon (which has become a canal, poor thing) join and the Jordan becomes one river!

In the past, the course of the Hermon River was used as a source of energy. Several flour mills were powered by it. One still operates on the Panyas site and the remains of the others can be seen when you walk from the east bank in the direction of the waterfall.

We have almost finished our stories about the Panyas, but all the memories and history almost made me forget to mention the wealth of vegetation to be seen here. We spoke of the huge plane tree which separates the two jets of the waterfall. It has some other relatives in the neighborhood, also lovers of streams, including a poplar and a nut tree. And we mustn't forget the willow. A little higher upstream there are other trees, among them several oaks. Hopefully they will not suffer the bitter fate of their brothers that were burned in the Tal Forest or at Tel Dan.

▶ The large waterfall at Nahal Hermon

Fierce Battles at Tel Faher —
MIZPE GOLANI (Golani Look-Out Post)

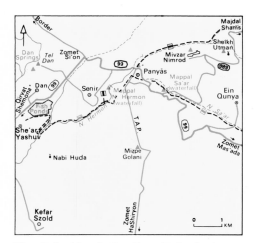

The Golani Look-Out Post (Tel Faher) stands at the side of the oil road — a road closed to both civilian and military traffic. Cars are permitted only on the section between Panyas and the Golani Look-Out Post. Set out from Panyas on Road 99 in the direction of the Golan. Next to the exit there's a road that connects with the oil road. To get to the site, drive along this road for about 2 kilometers in a general southerly direction.

This tour will take you to the western edge of the site and give you an opportunity to walk in trenches and look out from bunkers. You will return to Panyas using the same route.

The oil road, which serves as an approach to the site, was built parallel to the oil pipeline in order to guard it. The story of the oil pipeline suits the topsy-turviness of the Middle East: The pipeline, which belongs to "Aramco" (a joint Saudi-Arabian–American company), begins in the oilfields of the Persian Gulf. From there it meanders for a distance of 1,750 kilometers to the Mediterranean shore near the Lebanese town of Sidon. The oil pipeline was laid with the intention of circumventing Israel by going through the narrow pass between the Dan springs and Mount Hermon. But the Six Day War border changes brought some 50 kilometers of the pipeline inside Israeli territory. In 1968, the pipeline was sabotaged but it was repaired and oil continues to flow. In line with the contrariness of the Middle East, Arab-American oil flows through the Golan from Saudi-Arabia to Lebanon under the protection of Israel.

The pipeline is near Tel Faher, one of the Syrian fortifications that was captured by the Israel Defense Forces in the Six Day War. A fierce battle for this hill was fought mainly by the Golani Brigade and at the entrance to the site is a monument bearing the names of the Golani fallen. The name was changed after 1967 to the Golani Look-Out Post.

The battle for the hill began when a reinforced IDF troop, the "Barak" regiment, came uphill from the west. They attacked the horseshoe-shaped post frontally. (Visitors enter through the eastern opening.) About 100 meters in front of the barbed wire fences, the troop carriers that had managed to make their way were stopped. Twenty-five soldiers who survived the lethal Syrian fire charged and split the post in two, some heading for the southern target and some for the northern one, beyond the gorge. There were three fences between the men attacking the southern target and the trenches. One of the soldiers lay across the barbed wire while his friends jumped over him into the trenches and the bunkers. In the advance, most of the soldiers either died or were wounded — only three soldiers remained uninjured after the battle. But finally the southern target was almost entirely in the IDF's hands. The northern target was even more difficult to attain. Of the thirteen soldiers on the first wave of attack, only one was alive and uninjured at the end of the battle. Reinforcements were sent to this section of the post.

The regiment comander, who charged with the group that cleared out the trenches, was hit and killed. Most of the senior commanders of the force were wounded yet the men went on fighting bravely and stubbornly, meter by meter. The brigade's reconnaissance unit was rushed to the spot, and at dusk the target was finally taken. After this breakthrough all the other Syrian fortifications fell, and with them the entire Syrian line. The next day the Golani command post was in Kuneitra — in the heart of the Golan.

▲
Before it was covered with earth for security reasons, one of the valve-chambers of the oil pipeline looked like this

▶ The Golani Look-Out Post: a corner of the site

The Largest Ancient Synagogue in the Golan at
QAZRIN

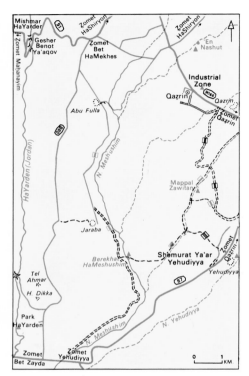

Access is very simple: The remains of the synagogue are near Qazrin, on Main Road 9088, near the industrial area.

▲
The gate of the Qazrin Synagogue prior to excavation

Qazrin today is the urban center of the Golan. A wide road leads into the settlement, first to the commercial center, with its office and other public buildings, and then to the residential area, the views and, on the outskirts of the settlement, to the Golan Field School. The industrial zone is situated outside the settlement, separated from it by the remains of a deserted Arab village built on ruins from the post-biblical period. The most outstanding of the remains are those of a synagogue. Around the synagogue and the oak trees which have survived is Qazrin Park. As at the other sites around the country, the proximity of the Muslim cemetery and the grave of a sheikh helped the oaks, especially the big one next to the synagogue building, survive.

There are remains of many synagogues in the Golan. The first were discovered as early as last century by Sir Lawrence Oliphant, who toured the Golan and thought of bringing Jews from Europe to settle there, and by Gustave Shumacher, who was looking for a route for a railroad from Damascus westwards to the Mediterranean. Some of the structures were excavated and there were clear signs that there had been a significant Jewish settlement here. After the Six Day War the remains of structures as well as single stones and inscriptions were found in many places in the Golan. One of the most important sites excavated was the Qazrin Synagogue, discovered as part of a 1968 survey. Today it is the most excavated, preserved, and visited structure in the Golan.

When the Qazrin Synagogue was first discovered, only the entrance and the arches beside it were noticeable. The ornamented portal and the architectural details, however, aroused "suspicion" and digging began. At the northern end of the remains a mosque had been built that cut across the synagogue. On the southern wall a stone with an Aramaic inscription was discovered. In the central building, measuring 5.40×18 meters, there was a hall with rows of benches. In the prayer hall there were rows of columns with Ionic-like capitals, similar to those found elsewhere in the Golan.

Various finds from the excavations are concentrated in the courtyard. The lintel over the gate is decorated with a narrow frieze flanked by pomegranates and jugs. There are also engravings of lamps, a gravestone with the inscription "Rabbi Avon lies in peace," a relief of a bird that looks like a peacock, and more. At the south of the synagogue remains of other buildings have been excavated, and all these together created an impressive complex of structures. Perhaps there was another public building here — a synagogue or a house of learning. Over the course of centuries the synagogue structure apparently underwent a change and at a certain stage it had a second storey.

The direction of the synagogue is different from the usual one. Most synagogue entrances were at the south, and those entering turned a complete circle in order to pray facing Jerusalem. In the Qazrin Synagogue the front and the entrance face north, and this gives us food for thought with regard to our ideas about the direction of prayer in ancient synagogues.

▶ The synagogue at Qazrin

A Town "Suspended in the Air" at
GAMLA

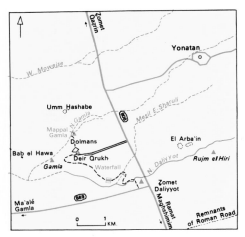

Road 808 branches off from Road 98 near Ramat Maghshimim, and ends at Road 87, which is the ascent from Yam Kinneret (Sea of Galilee) via Yehudiyya. Because it is near the waterfall it is also called "the waterfall road."
Some two kilometers north of Zomet Daliyyot (the junction of Roads 869 and 808) the road turns off to Nahal Daliyyot and the Gamla Reserve. The descent by foot to the Gamla site takes about 20 minutes and the climb up about 30 minutes. This is about the same time needed to reach Mappal Gamla, the waterfall, from the carpark.

▲
A view of Gamla from the memorial corner. The archaeological excavations are on the slope of the mountain

Beside the parking area there is a large signboard with a map. Stop here and consider what to do first. South of the carpark is the memorial to the first modern settlers of the Golan.

From the memorial there is an observation post over Gamla and the surroundings. The path from the carpark leads westwards towards Gamla. Looking down from the edge of the cliff you will see something odd: a fortified town, "a Massada of Galilee," not higher but much lower down than you are. A further look shows that Gamla stands on a steep spur between the Daliyyot and Gamla Rivers, and that it is accessible only from the direction of the cliff by which you descend.

Gamla was one of the fortified towns in Galilee and the Golan that held out in the revolt against the Romans in 66 C.E. The commander of Galilee was Joseph Ben Mattathias, later known as Josephus Flavius, and from his writings we learn about Gamla and other northern towns. After most of the Galilee and the Golan had fallen, the Romans besieged Gamla: "Gamla did not surrender, being even more secure than Yodefat in the natural fortifications of the place. For from a high mountain a rocky range slopes down, rising at its center to a hump. The slope from its peak is equal in its length from the front and the back, so that in shape the ridge resembles a camel [in Hebrew *gamal*] and this is how it got its name. Its two slopes and its face were steep from all sides, with impassable gorges, except for the tail end, where it is joined to the mountain . . . but even in this part the people of the town hindered access by digging a ditch . . . ."

For seven months the Romans besieged Gamla, attacking and retreating, and finally — after receiving reinforcements — they conquered it. According to historical sources, 4,000 Jewish fighters were killed here and 5,000 more threw themselves off the rocks to avoid being taken prisoner. But even if this number is highly exaggerated, it is difficult to tell how even a small number of town dwellers, refugees, and soldiers could have crushed together in so small a place on the steep slopes.

Archaeologists first thought another site was Gamla, and it was only in 1968, when a survey was made of the Golan, that this site was noticed and deemed a possibility. Excavations have now uncovered the remains of walls, a bath house, an aqueduct, a road of steps, an impressive synagogue, and houses that look like those described by Josephus: "The houses were built on the steep rib and they are joined together, so that one house fits onto another, and the town looks as if it is suspended in the air . . . ."

After visiting the site return using the same path you came down. Back at the start of the descent is the abandoned village of Dir-Karoach, with remains of a Byzantine structure and oil-press. To get to the Gamla Waterfall, continue on the path through the field of dolmens, which are table-like stone structures that were used in burials about 6,000 years ago. The path reaches as far as the riverside cliffs and will bring you to Gamla Waterfall. In terms of height, Israel's waterfalls are passable, but the quantities of water flowing over them do not come close to the world-famous falls. Gamla waterfall is 50 meters high — and it is the highest in the country. You can cross its course and walk some distance to look at it from the road to the Vultures' Look-Out.

► Gamla Waterfall

Beautiful Pillars and Water at
BEREKHAT HAMESHUSHIM (The Hexagonal Pool)

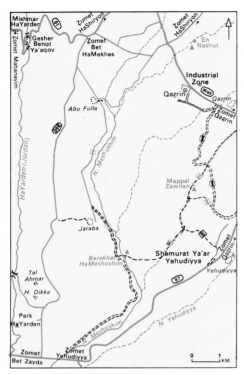

From Road 888, which connects what was once the upper Customs House with the Kinneret (Sea of Galilee) between kilometers 11-12, a road branches off in the direction of the Yehudiyya Forest and Berekhat HaMeshushim. After about six kilometers on this bad road, before you get to the ruins of the village Jerba, there is a small bridge. From here go on foot down a dirt road for two and one half kilometers, till you reach the path that leads to the river. The path is marked in red. ☐ **Some people are tempted to drive down the dirt road. This is not recommended.**
Return via the same route. It is possible to return via Road 87, which goes from Arik Bridge to the Golan, provided transportation is waiting there between kilometers 10-11. Some people try to drive up to the beginning of the path. This is very, very difficult.

The narrow road that branches off from Road 888 takes you past abandoned villages, agricultural land, and here and there water bubbling from a small spring. Below the road are green expanses and orchards once worked by Arab peasants. Not far from the road you can see the bubbling A-Dura spring. But stay on the road and go straight. From the other side of the stream, on the slope, you can see an irrigation canal which once brought the spring water to the fields. To the east of the road a forest stretches over an area of thousands of acres, mainly of Mt. Tabor oaks. This is the largest concentration of these oaks found in Israel.

This forest, or more specifically forest-park, is named for the abandoned village at its center — Yehudiyya. From various accounts, we know that in the past the forest was larger. It gradually dwindled to its present size, but after it was declared a nature reserve in 1973 the situation began to look up. The reserve is somewhat unusual and the shepherd, for example, through controlled grazing of his flock, helps to preserve the forest .... Surplus gazelles were brought to the reserve from Ramot Issaschar. As in the days of creation of the world, they saw it was good, were fruitful, and multiplied ... and today their numbers have grown so large as to constitute a threat to their own existence. The local farmers are up in arms against them. It appears that the gazelles are not only beautiful, swift, and delicate; they also eat — and this arrangement is not to the liking of the farmers, who claim that their crops are not intended precisely for gazelles ...

There are all kinds of trees and other animals in the reserve. There are also natural sites (e.g., Nahal Zavitan and Berekhat HaMeshushim), and of course flora peculiar to the streams which cut through the basalt level of the Yehudiyya Reserve.

Turn on to the dirt road and walk parallel to the course of Nahal Meshushim. The road slopes gently downward and was designed, before it was ruined, for vehicles of all types.

Down by the river the path is hidden under thick vegetation. When the path forks go to the left, through the thick brush. A five-minute walk will bring you to a small waterfall. Here, cross the stream carefully and continue along the eastern bank above the waterfall, to a bridge over a basalt canyon, and from there to the observation post above the pool.

From the observation post you can discern hundreds of basalt pillars which form the pool and the stream leading to it — grey-black columns with five and six sides. But when you go down to the pool you'll find that only the "heads" of the pillars are visible; it is as though the surface were meticulously paved with pentagonal and hexagonal tiles. The pillars are actually the solidified lava that flowed here in the past. On cooling, lava contracts into polygons.

On a trip to the United States we were somewhat disappointed when we saw five and six-sided basalt pillars, and then we read that there are lots of others all over the world. But the Golan pillars are still special — they come in various types, and more important, in the Golan they stand in the water — and you can, too. After bathing return by the same path to the dirt road.

▶ The road to Berekhat HaMeshushim. In the background: Yehudiyya Forest Park

▶ Hexagonal Pool, Berekhat HaMeshushim

UPPER GALILEE, THE HULA VALLEY, GALILEE COAST

Until the 1930s, Upper Galilee was "unexplored territory." Its height, vegetation, and manner in which it is divided, and its paucity of roads made it almost impassable. In the distant past Israelites settled here, finding it for the most part sparsely populated. Throughout the centuries, it served as a refugee for various communities, including Druse, Christians, Cherkassians, and Mograbis all of whom came here, sometimes fleeing each other in their countries of origin. It is not by chance that Upper Galilee was called "Galilee of the Nations."

When the "Northern" road was built by the British it served, along with some other roads, as a kind of entrance into Galilee. When Israel was established, Jewish settlement was sparse in Upper Galilee and those responsible for settlement tried to change its demography. Lake Hula in the east was drained, and new settlements were set up on the northern border and in the central Galilee. Roads were cut through to the settlements — both border roads and highways. And the treasures of Galilee were opened up.

The Mount Meron area offers many beautiful sports and hiking routes on its peaks. At its base are the Ammud and Keziv Rivers. Natural vegetation, flowing streams and magnificent hilltop views are among the many attractions. Here are the remains of ancient settlements, synagogues, fortresses, and medieval castles. Neither Mount Meron itself, nor the Upper Ammud River and the Birya Forests, nor even the Hula Reserve are included in this book. Even so, it is no mere chance that Upper Galilee takes up so considerable a portion of this book.

Paradise and Legends at
TEL DAN

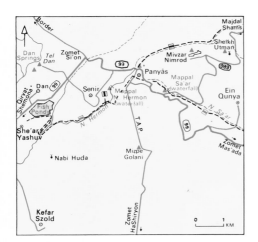

Take Road 99 eastwards from Qiryat Shemona. Go past the Tal Forest and Kibbutz Dan, and about one kilometer after the kibbutz (between kilometers 9-10) turn left onto a road leading to a carpark. At the entrance you can buy a very useful folder with a map marking the stations.

Let's get one thing clear from the start: Swimming at Tel Dan is difficult if not impossible. Dan springs are in the Hermon and that should give you some indication of the temperature of the water. Once upon a time, before the area was declared a nature reserve, the main attractions of the site were the flour mills and the pool. There were he-men who took dips in this cold water and some even braver souls who actually tried to swim. The length of a dip in the cold waters became the subject of bets. And the word cold is an understatement . . . freezing is more accurate! Most of the challengers would jump into the water quickly and jump out even faster. The daring young man who stayed in a few minutes became a hero, and whoever stayed in longer — well, weeks after the trip he would still be shivering in the heat of summer. Today the mills are inoperative and swimming is not allowed. But, there is another place where you can swim in equally cold water — the Tal Forest pool. Go ahead and try it.

Something about the Dan River itself. It is the largest of the three tributaries which form the Jordan. It is also the only one which has always been inside Israel's border (unlike the Snir which is in Lebanon and the Hermon which was in Syrian territory). The Dan supplies about half of the Jordan waters and because of its profuse flow it is also called "The Little Jordan." It is difficult to identify the Dan because of the presence of many streams and rivulets and artificial canals. Several springs supply the Dan, including Ein Dan, Ein Laish (as in the name of the town before it was captured by the tribe of Dan), and Ein Leshem. Hundreds of years ago irrigation canals were dug in the area. As a result of neglect vegetation covered their banks, and now it is difficult to distinguish between them and the natural streams.

Just as in other places with streaming water, there was a flour mill here, powered by one of the streams of the Dan. The mill belonged to Abed-A-Salim of Shaba'a Village, which was north of the Dan, and most of its customers came from the Syrian villages near the border. For many years the mill was abandoned; when the paths of the nature reserve were opened, it was restored, but only for show.

Today the reserve is skirted by an open area with tables and benches for resting and eating al fresco. Inside the reserve is a network of signposted paths that take the visitor easily from place to place. Trees are identified by name so that pleasure can be combined with a little learning. There are Syrian ash, and laurel with many ferns, buckthorn, oak and pistachio. — and if I write all their names it will fill the entire page. In any case, what difference do names make? (Yes, there are also the more familiar eucalyptus and poplars). There is also a paradise, and when you get to the edge of the reserve you will find it — bubbling, streaming water, the whisper of leaves, and a patch of sky through the treetops. And there is also a mound with interesting archaeological excavations: A gate, an entrance to a town, walls, buildings, perhaps even the temple which competed with Solomon's after the kingdom was split . . . .

Once the archaeological mound was called Tel-el-Kadi (the Hill of the Judge). *Kadi* is judge in Arabic, like *dayan* and *dan* in Hebrew and perhaps this is the reason for the name. There are legends, too — one of which tells of a judge who sat here solving the problems of the streams of the Jordan, which quarrelled among themselves for leadership. But . . . all the stories and legends cannot compare with the sight before you. This is one of Israel's gems of nature, especially the spot that may truly be called paradise.

▲
The remains of the temple at the Tel Dan excavations

▶ The flow of the Dan River near Tel Dan

Were the Trees Once Really Stakes in
HORESHAT TAL (Tal Forest)?

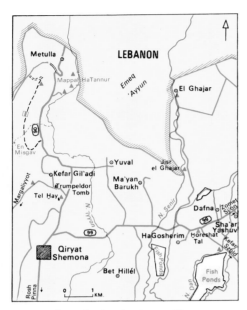

Getting here is simple. From Qiryat Shemona drive eastward on Road 99. If you've passed Kibbutz HaGoshrim you're getting close. If you've reached Dafna, Dan, or Sha'ar Yashuv — then you have to go back a bit, to between kilometers 5-6.

▲
Burnt-out tree in Horeshat Tal

When can one swim in Horeshat Tal? It's hard to say. In winter who of us would dare go into any pool, let alone a pool filled with the freezing waters of the Dan? In summer, it's hot outside, and cold in the waters, and the contrast in temperature takes your breath away .... Still, a dip in the waters in Horeshat Tal is highly recommended on any trip north.

Israelis used to call it the Forest of the Forty, undeterred by the fact that the Forest of the Forty is on the Carmel Mountain Range. The number forty is sacred to the Muslims and appears in many places. It is associated with the disciples of the Prophet Mohammed who, among other things, accompanied him on his journeys. No one knows who gave the place its name. The more pedantic called it the Forest of Ten, and in fact this is its Arabic name: Sajarat-El-Asarah or Sajarat-Sheikh-Ali, or the Sheikh Ali Forest. The story behind the name is repeated with minor variations about several places in Israel. It tells of ten of Mohammed's friends who, on their way from Mecca, cut across the length of Palestine. When they reached this spot, they dismounted. As there were no trees in the area to serve as posts, they drove stakes into the ground and tied their horses to them. After resting and drinking the cool water of the stream, they mounted their horses and rode on their way, but . . . the stakes remained. Soon the stakes struck roots, and grew and grew until they became tall trees .... How did ten stakes grow into a forest with hundreds of trees? Well, perhaps they were only ten riders, but their large caravan of beasts would of course require many stakes. But let's not argue with legends.

So much for the name Forest of Ten. The other name, Sajarat-Sheikh-Ali, is connected with a sheikh whose nearby grave was a lodestone to Arab residents of the Hula Valley, and who came here on pilgrimages. Thanks to his grave, this forest (as well as others in Israel) was preserved from harm and from tree-felling. The dominant tree in the forst is the Mt. Tabor oak and it certainly does not disgrace the saying, "strong as an oak." There are trees here that are hundreds of years old with trunks so broad that it takes several people to encircle them. Near the forest, and inside it, flow streams of the Dan River, and the abundance of water and trees have made it one of the most beautiful spots in the area. Among the trees are picnic areas, open patches of grass, and a large pool filled with the very cold waters of the Dan.

Wander around the park and along its paths. There is an oak that was hit by lightning in 1952. The inside of the trunk burned but the tree did not collapse. It still stands at the entrance to the park drawing the attention of visitors. There are about 240 oak trees that are between 350 and 400 years old. We should add that only half of Horeshat Tal is a national park open to us; the other half — a nature reserve — is closed to the public.

We almost forgot: The source of the Hebrew name, Horeshat Tal, is Psalm 133:3, which hints at the proximity of the Hermon: "Like the dew [tal] of the Hermon which falls on the hills of Zion."

To the south-east of Horeshat Tal is an orchid reserve. The best time to visit there is in March. Come with an orchid expert if you can.

▶ Horeshat Tal — on the horizon the snows of the Hermon

Once They Lined Up for Days at
MAPPAL HATACHANA (the Mill Fall)

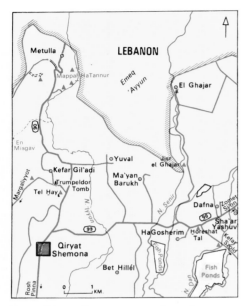

From Qiryat Shemona travel north on Road 90 to Metulla. At the entrance to Metulla near kilometer 478 a narrow road turns east and leads to a look-out point from which you can see the Mill Fall. You can go down to the river from here, or from a foot path at the north end of Metulla, which goes down to Nahal Ayyon and passes several waterfalls before it reaches Mappal Hatannur, the Tannur Fall. Details can be obtained from the Nature Reserves Authority official at the carpark at the entrance to the Tannur, which can be reached by turning off Road 90 between kilometers 476-477.

If it is summer, the chances are that you will see little if any water. In spring, however, there is an abundance of water and flowers. The water story is about rainfall, melting snows "in the neighborhood," and the irrigation arrangements of Lebanese farmers across the border. Nahal Ayyon drains Emeq Ayyun (the Ayyun Valley), where there are fields and cultivated land watered by the springs that also supply our waterfalls.

The Ayyon River, formerly known by its Arabic name, Bara'it, drains the southern Ayyon Valley. Once it flowed into the Hula swamps, but then — its waters began to stagnate in the thick vegetation of the swamps and its course disappeared before reaching the Jordan. Today it makes its way via one of the drainage canals of the valley.

The Mill Fall is about halfway between the northern carpark and the Tannur. The waterfall is named for the flour mill whose remains can be clearly seen. Water fell here from a height of 15 meters into a canal cut into the rock. This brought some of the water to the vents of the mill, which moved the turbine that turned an axle attached to the mill-stones that ground the flour. The mill belonged to a Druse family even before Metulla was built. When the township was established the Jewish inhabitants repaired and began operating it. On the researcher Lunz's *Calendar of Palestine* for the year 1896, it says: "And there are already good stone houses built, water-mills which will bring income." The township used to lease the mill to one of the settlers, who worked it together with a resident of the nearby Lebanese village of El-Hayam. It was operative only five months a year, while the river flowed. Before World War I operation ceased and at the end of the war it was given to one of the Jewish residents of Metulla on condition that he repair it. The wooden water wheels were replaced with iron ones and the output of the mill doubled. The mill served the residents of Metulla and many Lebanese villages. Sometimes villagers waited their turn at the mill for a day, two days, and even more. In 1920, the mill stopped and has never been used again. It was replaced by a more sophisticated mill at the nearby township of Gedidah. All that remains of the mill is part of the structure and the name it gave to the waterfall.

From the waterfall, continue walking on the path hewn into the rock by the people of Metulla to provide access to the pumping station. It can be seen to the west of the path beyond the riverbed. The next waterfall is the Eshed Fall, from which you can climb stone steps to a path at the edge of the cliff. At the other side of the river are niches in which rock doves make their nests, side by side with their enemies, the falcons. The path ends near the Metulla cemetery. From here go down to a better-known waterfall — the Tannur — which the Arabs thought resembled an oven. The Hebrew word for oven is *tannur,* and even though the fall was once also called *Nukvata Dayun*, the Ayyon tunnel, the name Tannur stuck.

If you come in the right season there will be raspberry bushes, willow trees, michauxia, snapdragons, and many other flowers.

▲
A view of Nahal Ayyon

▶ The Mill Fall

The Connection Between the 11th of Adar and the Galilee Panhandle in Tales of
TEL HAY

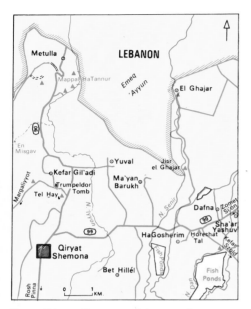

From Qiryat Shemona drive north on Road 90. Between Tel Hay and Kefar Gil'adi Road 9977 turns west towards Margaliot; at the junction there is a small road leading off to the left to Tel Hay. A little further along on Road 9977, to the left, is the entrance to the youth hostel, a little further on to the right (at kilometer 81) is the turnoff to the Statue of the Roaring Lion.

▲
Part of the Tel Hay courtyard

On a hill visible from the north of the Hula Valley is the Ha-Shomer Organization cemetery. Among the graves stands a famous, Roaring Lion. The statue, executed by the sculptor Melnikov, is 6 meters tall; inscribed at its base are Joseph Trumpeldor's legendary last words, "It is good to die for our country," and the names of those who fell at Tel Hay.

In the courtyard the development of Jewish settlement in Galilee can be traced. Inside a special room is devoted to Trumpeldor. On display are documents about his life and activities, and also weapons used by the residents of Galilee from the time Tel Hay was established up to the War of Independence. Youth activities are held here in the spirit of those early pioneering days: Flour is ground and baked in the antiquated ovens, and there is even an exercise in setting up a tower and stockade in the style of the settlements of that period . . . .

In 1919-1920, by force of the famous Sykes-Picot agreement signed between the British and the French during World War I, this part of the country was put under the French sphere of influence, and most of the rest of the country under the British. The problems of dividing the region were complicated by the intervention of the Emir Feisal, who represented the Arabs who had fought with the British in the war. Feisal demanded Syria, and included a part of Upper Galilee that was the home of several Jewish settlements — Hamra, Metulla, Kefar Gil'adi, and Tel Hay.

Most Jewish settlement at the time was concentrated in the south of the country and communications were difficult. The Jews of these northern settlements found themselves unwilling partners to the play of forces between the French and the Arabs. Chaos prevailed in the area. And through it all Arab bands attacked Tel Hay several times. There were people here who had "volunteered for the frontier" in the phrase of those days. The enclosed courtyard shielded the poorly-armed volunteers during the attacks, but it did not hold out in the heaviest attack, which came on the 11th of Adar, 1920.

The canal that brought water from Kefar Gil'adi to Tel Hay had become blocked the night before the attack. When morning came, Joseph Trumpeldor, recently appointed commander of Tel Hay, went off to Kefar Gil'adi with his friends to unblock the canal. After they left a large band of Arabs led by Kamal Effendi arrived. They had come, they said, to look for French soldiers who had taken cover in Tel Hay. They shot into the air to punctuate their demands and the sounds brought Trumpeldor and his colleagues rushing back from Kefar Gil'adi. In the meanwhile, however, Kamal and his men broke through to an upper room in the farmhouse — the only building in Tel Hay that had a second floor — and from there opened fire on the people in the courtyard. Others of Kamal's men encircled the settlement. After a while, when the defenders were spread out though still fighting bravely, the attackers took advantage of the situation and left the yard. Trumpeldor was severely wounded in the stomach and died.

The people of Tel Hay gathered their dead and wounded and moved to Kefar Gil'adi. Later they infiltrated to the British area further south. Eight men and women lost their lives at Tel Hay during this and previous attacks, and this is the origin of the name of the neighboring town of Qiryat Shemona, which means the town of eight.

Tel Hay and the other Jewish settlements in the area were abandoned but the heroic stand of the settlers left its mark. When the Palestine Mandatory borders were finally established, this part of Galilee was included in the British sphere of influence that was designated to be a National Home for the Jews in the Land of Israel.

▶ The "Roaring Lion," by Melnikov, in the Tel Hay cemetery

War on Malaria and Silkworms at
ROSH PINNA

The end of Road 89 is actually Rosh Pinna's main street. It joins Road 90 near the gas station, the restaurants, the police station, and the hitch-hiking station to Upper Galilee and the Golan.

▲
A cobbled road in Rosh Pinna

There are some who say they visited Rosh Pinna if they passed through on their way from Tiberias to Qiryat Shemona or the Golan, or on their way to Zefat. For many soldiers and hitch-hikers Rosh Pinna is the "junction at the bottom." In the past there was a customs post here (old-timers in Galilee will bear witness), and under British rule anyone who went to the Galilee panhandle, to Syria via the Benot Ya'aqov Bridge, went through a customs check here.

The main road, which is a part of Road 89, is the lower road of the village, the "Teverya Road," from which people went to Tiberias. But the real Rosh Pinna is not this strip of road. The real Rosh Pinna is the upper road which is the road of the founders, where it all began.

The story begins in 1877, when a number of families from Zefat bought land from the Arabs of the Ja'uni Village and tried to establish the Jewish village "Gei Oni." Some years later the representative of a group of Rumanian Jews explored and examined the place, bought land, and in 1882 several score families came here from Rumania. The name of the place, so it is told, was chosen because of the many stones they found on their land. According to the Book of Psalms, "The stone rejected by the builders became the cornerstone," and indeed this place became a cornerstone, which is the translation of the name Rosh Pinna. Among local professions and sources of livelihood in the past were tobacco growing and . . . producing silk from silkworms. Baron Rothschild encouraged the planting of mulberry trees and many stories are told about the silkworms and the larvae that every farmer received to start off the new industry. As the years passed, the region was abandoned and the houses lay in ruins. Here and there people on that fringe squatted in some of the houses; then Rosh Pinna's hidden treasures were discovered.

Today the village has a new lease on life. A restoration project was established and has begun to return the village to its former glory.

You will get into the mood as soon as you start going up the old street cobbled in the style of yesteryear. Up above, on Founders Street, the PICA House (Palestinian Jewish Colonial Association) has been repaired. This house, which served the clerks of Baron Rothschild and was partially destroyed, has become an exhibition center and the home of the Rosh Pinna College for the Study of Settlement in Galilee. It is also the center for the restoration works. In a cave beneath the building is a memorial to Shlomo Ben-Yosef, who was hanged by the British in 1938. The house next door belonged to Professor Mar and it was here that his laboratory and center for the war on malaria was located. Further up the street is the synagogue built in 1882, the remains of the Schwartz Hotel, the Hazbani Levy family house, and so on.

Rosh Pinna's location on the main road, the view from it of the Hula Valley and the Hermon, and the restoration of Founders Street make this a must for travelers.

▶ A view of some of the old houses of Rosh Pinna

A Meeting with Pretty Girls at
NAHAL AVIV (Aviv River)

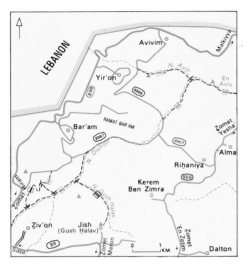

Road 8966 is the rear road between Kibbutz Yir'on and Moshav Avivim. It branches off from the north road near Avivim. Between kilometers 4-5 there is a bend in the road. At the north side of the bend there are blue markings on the roadside, and these will accompany you on your tour of Nahal Aviv.
It takes about 30 minutes to get from the road to the "girls."

▲
Caves at Nahal Aviv

Do you want to know the "girls'" exact names? For starters, we'll stick to their address — Nahal Aviv — southern bank, about 200 meters east of the outlet of the sewage-filled course coming from the direction of Yir'on. This is enough of a signpost. Just go down the blue-marked path ▭ that begins at Road 8966. As usually happens in life, your path in pursuit of the "girls" will not be strewn with roses. Skip from stone to stone of the rocky riverbed formed by the building of the road. Don't let the jumping deny you the opportunity to look around and notice that the "girls" live in beautiful and dignified surroundings. Here and there you can see a canyon or a cliff above, and the road is delightful. This is some consolation in case you don't succeed with the "girls." The name of the "street" you are walking along is Nahal Aviv. This is not its original name. The Arabs call it Wadi Uba, the name they also give to the large spring near where it joins Nahal Dishon. Apparently in the past the "girls" had problems and they frequently changed the name of the river where they lived. Perhaps they were trying to get rid of pests. The river also has other names in Arabic and in Hebrew, too; on some maps it is called Nahal Avivim.

Right near the "girls" you will be filled with joy at the sound of running water. A flowing stream! What a treat. But when you get closer you will see that this is not exactly what one would call running water. To be on the safe side drink from your canteens . . . .

At last you arrive. The "girls" rise up on the southern bank above you. Leave the blue-marked path here and ascend by any path you find. There are three "girls" here. A little further on there are a few more, and you can visit them all. As for their names, I'm afraid I don't have much to say. I heard them called "pretty girls" — but I'm not sure if this is a description or their name? Hikers simply call them "girls," although the three together are sometimes called "the three aunts." I do have some authoritative information about their anatomy though, and here it is: "The shape of the rock is a phenomenon caused by the splitting of the mother rock, by narrow, deep and dense cracks. The depth of the cracks reaches two meters and more . . . . The differences in resistance to dissolution cause the formation of giant rocks, hollow inside and resembling columns 8-9 meters tall, such as those that have survived on the slopes of Nahal Aviv . . . ." This is a description by two geologists who studied the region, so now everything should be clear. The rock girls are made of soft (lovely!) rock and they survived when everything around them was swept away. They were protected by their caps of harder rock. Our pretty girls, we must remark, are partially hollow. That's life . . . . Here and there you can stand in the shade of one of them or even (Heavens!) climb inside their hollow bodies and pose for a photograph . . . at their heads, for example.

Return the way you came, or — since you are already up here — cut across to the road, avoiding the river course descending from Yir'on. Incidentally, further up the river there are attractive rocks, an interesting cave, a network of carved tunnels, and in the right season (mostly spring) — flowers (in November there are sternberrings that are worth all the effort). Sometimes you also meet birds of prey, hyraxes, and gazelles at the river. But don't take this as a promise. It's a matter of luck . . . .

▶ The "pretty girls" at Nahal Aviv

Queen Esther and Two Synagogues at
BAR'AM

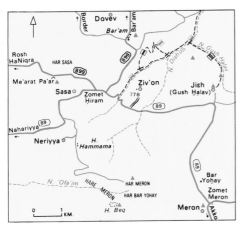

At Zomet Hiram (the Hiram Junction) near Sasa, take Road 89 (Nahariyya – Ma'alot – Meron). Follow the road that branches off (a continuation of Road 899) for two kilometers and you will be at the entrance to Bar'am.

Bar'am (formerly Bir'im) is a Maronite border village that was almost entirely destroyed in the War of Independence. What remains today is the Maronite church, looked after by one of the village families, the graveyard at the edge of the village, and the repaired Jewish synagogue. Remains of arches and parts of buildings can be seen, with some of the stones in secondary use from more ancient buildings that stood here.

There are several traditions connected with the village and one of them claims that Queen Esther is buried here. An anonymous author, a student of Nahmanides, who traveled in the country in the fourteenth century, describes important graves, and writes, "Near there is Queen Esther. The mouth of the cave is at the top, and a large stone covers its mouth." Some one hundred years later Moses Bassoula wrote that there was a heap of stones and an oak tree beside Esther's grave. There is a painting depicting a gravestone with a tree beside it in the book, *Genealogy of the Fathers and the Prophets,* that dates from 1536.

Today there is no sign of Esther's grave at Bar'am, although there are those who point to a sign of the grave not far from the site, at the fringes of the Bar'am forest. Other famous personalities are also connected with Bar'am and with its two ancient synagogues. One of these synagogues was described to early travelers as Obadiah's synagogue or as a synagogue close to the grave of Obadiah the Prophet. A lintel with the inscription from this synagogue is in the Louvre Museum in Paris. Nineteenth-century explorers saw the doorway of this synagogue, which was apparently located at the east of the village, and painted it. The second synagogue has come down to us from the third century C.E., and is one of the most beautiful and impressive in Israel. The splendor of this synagogue was noted hundreds of years ago. Thirteenth- and fourteenth-century travelers wrote of it: "The synagogue is very beautiful" and "There in the village is a synagogue . . . a very splendid building. Large overlaid stones and broad long pillars. I have never seen such a splendid building." The synagogue was excavated at the beginning of this century, but the main preservation and cleaning were done more recently.

On entering the synagogue from the square one confronts a majestic facade, which faces south to Jerusalem. There are three entrances at the front, a large one in the center, its lintel decorated with vines and clusters of grapes. The dedicatory inscription in Aramaic tells that the building was sponsored by "the son of Eliezer ben Yodan." The synagogue structure is rectangular, and through the gate is the prayer hall, which was divided by rows of columns into a central hall and colonnades formed beyond the pillars built in a U-shape. In the corners of the hall are heart-shaped columns, like those found in other early synagogues discovered in Israel. The ceiling apparently rested on the pillars, and perhaps there was another storey. The floor of the synagogue was made of stone slabs, some of which have been preserved.

From the square beside the synagogue there is an excellent view, and on a clear winter day "Grandfather Hermon" with its snow-capped head can be seen.

▲
The synagogue at Bar'am

▶ **The entrance to the synagogue at Bar'am**

Close to Zefat There Is a Place Called
MERON

Take Road 866, which branches off about half a kilometer before Zomet Meron (the Meron Junction), and turn on to the road which goes up to the grave of Rabbi Shimon Bar Yohai and the neighboring buildings.

The view does not always look like it does in the photograph, which was taken on the holiday of Lag Ba'Omer at the grave of Rabbi Shimon Bar Yohai, and is what accounts for the bonfires, feasting, and celebration. The view has not changed much for centuries; in a description written in the eighteenth century we read: "And about two hours [by foot] from Zefat there is a place called Meron. Here is the cave of Rabbi Shimon Bar Yohai and his son Elazar and over the cave is a large handsome building with all kinds of paintings. Three times a year they go from all the places in the Land of Israel to his grave ... and once on Lag Ba'Omer .... This is called the festival of Rabbi Shimon. And they have a tradition from ancient times, that on that day they have to make merry and hold big feasts with drums and dancing and everything possible."

The celebration begins with the taking of the Scrolls of the Law in a grand procession from synagogues in Zefat and bringing them to Meron. Once the procession arrives, it's almost impossible to see anything. There are thousands of people celebrating, a full carpark, and the very real danger of being crushed on the way to the grave of Rabbi Shimon.

The central building at the site has a number of wings, a yard, and steps up to the roof. It is built over the grave of Rabbi Shimon and his son Elazar. About 1,700 years ago the famous exponent of the Talmud and his son fled the Romans and hid in this cave for many years. According to tradition, it was during this period that Rabbi Shimon Bar Yohai wrote the Zohar, the major work of Jewish mysticism.

In the left wing are passages to prayer rooms and a small library. Standing out from the wall is part of the gravestone of Rabbi Shimon. Here people pray, place notes with various requests for intercession, and light candles. In the central hall is the grave of Elazar and at the side, beyond a lattice, the grave of Rabbi Shimon. This room is *the* attraction. It has a domed roof and close to the dome are beacon poles, one named for Shimon and the other for Elazar. Here on Lag Ba'Omer torches are lit and the beacons are carried up amid prayers and dancing.

Other sages are buried around the graves of Shimon and Elazar, among them possibly Hillel the Elder and his pupils. There are other graves above the central structure, and to the north, on a hillock, there are the remains of an ancient synagogue. This synagogue is among the largest found in Galilee and its structure recalls other synagogues in the area. It is about 1,700 years old. The roots of Meron are even older: it is mentioned in the records of Egyptian kings who invaded the land of Israel more than 3,000 years ago. Much later it is noted as one of the fortresses of Josephus Flavius who fortified Galilee against the Romans.

Why do people come here particularly on Lag Ba'Omer? Lag Ba'Omer is the thirty-third day between the festivals of Passover and Pentecost. Some say it is a day of mourning in memory of the destruction of the Temple, to which harvest offerings were once but could no longer be brought; some say it is a day of mourning for Bar Kokheva and his warriors who failed in their revolt against the Romans; some say it marks the end of the mourning period — when there was a turn in favor of the rebels. The day is also remembered as the turning point in the great plague that spread among the students of Rabbi Akiva, in which 24,000 pupils are said to have died. But people come to Meron on Lag Ba'Omer mainly because it is said to be the day on which Rabbi Shimon Bar Yohai died and entered paradise. They come to honor the great rabbi, and while they are here they picnic and go out into the forests and shoot bows and arrows.

A tree beside one of the graves at Meron. The scraps of cloth are signs left by pilgrims.

▶ Meron on Lag Ba'Omer

A Cave without a Roof and a Bridge in the Air at
ME'ARAT KESHET (Keshet Cave)

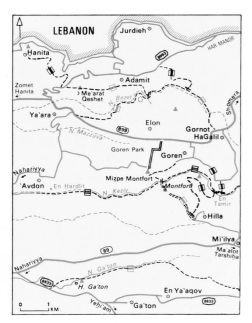

Turn from Road 4 near the coast, onto Road 899, the north road. Between kilometers 6-7 Road 8993 turns off and climbs towards Adamit. Between kilometers 2-3 a path marked in red leads to Me'arat Keshet.

The entire route to Keshet Cave, beginning on the north road, is scenic; the view begins at the start of the ascent to Adamit. Until this road was paved, Adamit was as good as out of the country. It is bounded to the south and the east by the deep bed of Nahal Bezet, to the west by Nahal Namer, and to the north by Lebanon. In point of fact, it was easier to reach Adamit from Lebanon than from Israel. When the road was built about 20 years ago, the Arab-El-Aramsha Bedouin tribe (once alone in the area) suddenly found itself living a new life style.

The road clings to the sides of the mountain as it climbs upward. After less than a kilometer, at the first bend, Nahal Namer and the open caves on its cliffs come into view. There is a reason the river is is called Namer (dalem in Arabic and leopard in English): Some 30 years ago a leopard was caught here! And about 20 years ago a Bedouin shepherd achieved instant fame when he encountered another leopard — and the victor of the battle that ensued was no other than the one who lived to tell the tale. Since then, no leopards have been seen at the river, but who knows . . . ?

Despite the story of the leopards, you can park at one of the bends and go down to have a look at the river. Then continue driving up and stop near the beginning of the path marked in red. Don't confuse this with the path marked in black which also goes down to Nahal Namer but to a stalactite cave — which is another story.

Take the red path, climb up a crag (these few meters are the hardest part of the trip; the rest of the path is easier). From the path there are wonderful views on all sides. Part of it crosses a rocky area, full of boulders and another part is right on the edge of the cliff facing Nahal Bezet. Pause here to look at the view and the steep cliffs. After about 20-30 minutes you will reach Keshet Cave. This cave came into being like all other caves, with water seeping below the ground surface, dissolving the rock, and creating cavities, spaces, and tunnels of different depths. Many caves appear on mountainsides at river banks; when the river cuts its way through the hill the wall of the opening is eroded and the cave is formed. But Keshet Cave has an additional story — its roof collapsed, leaving only a strip of rock as a kind of bridge. Look over the bridge at the villages of Galilee and under the bridge at the view of Nahal Bezet. In Hebrew, *Keshet* means arc, and it is not difficult to understand how the cave got its name.

The red path which goes east from Keshet Cave leads first to the heights and then goes down to Nahal Bezet and meets it at this beautiful spot.

A cliff above Nahal Bezet on the way to Keshet Cave

One Kilometer of Beauty at
NAHAL BEZET (Bezet River)

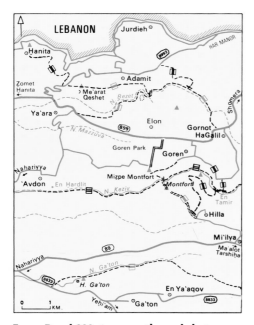

From Road 899, turn northwards between kilometers 10-11 near Kibbutz Elon. Go down the road leading from the kibbutz to the pumps at the river. Access is possible only to small vehicles, or individuals on foot. From the pumps go up the river a short way until you get to the huge plane trees .... You can't miss it!

Looking from above, from the northern heights, the view is much like a forest — rich and genuine Galilee green. And the world below, in the gorges and cliffs, is also painted in magnificent hues of green. From April through August, it is also pink and flowing with water, and much more .... Once we called it by its Arabic name, Karkara, and "I've come back from Karkara" would cause a speaker's eyes to light up. The map still lists the name, Springs of Karkara, but the river's Arabic name derives from ruins of buildings, oil-presses, and the mosaic floor of a fifth-century church found here. The Karkara River (Bezet) is the northernmost river in Israel's coastal area. And despite the fact that it flows in geological and climatic conditions similar to its neighbors, it is nevertheless different from them — and better.

There are all kinds of good things to be found in its tributaries and in its main course: hyraxes that you will meet (if you're quiet and lucky), cliffs, caves, thick woods on the slopes, and flowing water in a short but impressive section. There are large plane trees and many, many oleanders. City dwellers once called these oleanders "lice trees" because their leaves were covered with insects. The oleander, which blossoms from April through August, paints the river in bold colors. In the section where the water flows there is a web of oleander through which you can walk and in the riverbed and beside the huge plane trees there are ferns, among them maidenhair, which is probably better known than the others. For most of its length, for most of the year, the river is dry, flowing with rain water only in winter. But the section we are referring to streams all year and is supplied by springs. It flows alongside the bank for a distance of about 1,500 meters until it is caught by the pumps of Kibbutz Elon and makes its way up through iron pipes for multi-purpose use.

In the past this spring water was used to power several flour mills. The remains of conduits branching off to the mills are still discernible. One conduit reaches a mill which was operated by a man from the village of Mi'ilya. There were mills at Nahal Keziv, closer to his home, but this man invested in an operation further afield. He leased the mills and apparently the income from them was not bad. In summer only one mill worked. No water, no flour ....

A path marked in blue ▭ coming down from Adamit and up the Sherach River to the north road, crosses the Bezet. There are other hiking possibilities here, but even if you go east from the pumps of Kibbutz Elon alongside the pipe, you will want to stop, admire, and enjoy the charming spots along the course of the river.

▲
Walking through the thicket at Nahal Bezet

▶ Nahal Bezet — a view from Adamit Heights

You Won't Be Disappointed at
NAHAL KEZIV (Keziv River)

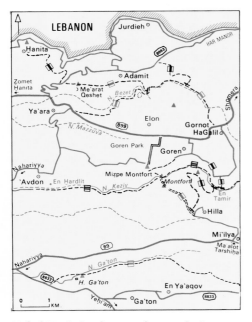

Nahal Keziv is a long and meandering river. This visit will be to the stretch between En Tamir and the foot of the Montfort. There are several routes: (a) From the north road, 899, turn off between kilometers 11-12 to Goren Park, and from there, at the Montfort look-out post, go down on foot to the river and up its course (eastwards); (b) from Road 89 between kilometers 15-16 turn in the direction of Montfort, go down on foot towards Montfort, and from there to the river. There are other possibilities which can be found on a hiking map of the marked trails of Upper Galilee.

▲
Pools at Nahal Keziv

The upper streams of Nahal Keziv are on the slopes of Mount Meron, high in the Galilee. In the river's lower course, there are several springs trapped in pumprooms and one that is still entirely free. This section is incredibly beautiful, which is not meant to deny the beauty of other parts of the river, but still . . . .

True, a dirt road spans the entire stretch, and dusty jeeps sometimes spoil its rustic beauty — but what can we do? The struggle for the road and the water began when it was decided to trap all the springs of the river. In 1952, En Ziv (Ras-A-Naba in Arabic, meaning, the fountainhead, and this spring is indeed the river's main source) was caught, then another spring, En Hardalit, was caught further west. When it was decided to join the two "captives" and expand the water project, the idea of a road in the riverbed was born. A cry went up, nature lovers sprang into battle, and something was saved: The road was paved carefully to avoid harming the landscape and another small spring which had been in danger of annexation, En Tamir, was left free . . . . In addition, water was allocated for maintaining the woodland (yes, water to irrigate the trees!). Cooperation of the best sort: A natural resource was developed and something of this rare natural beauty was left untouched.

Hyraxes, frogs, fowl, fish, and here and there birds of prey — they are all here, all in motion, all fleeing from guests they do not always welcome. Only the many flour mills and trees do not run away. The history of most of the flour mills ended when Israel was established. Gone are the days when farmers made their way to these water-powered mills to grind their flour, meet with neighbors, and exchange a little gossip about other villagers and the big world beyond.

Among the trees, the plane trees are dominant. Those that grew in parts of the river deprived of water suffered. At one time they had stretched along the river for a distance of over ten kilometers! What we have left today is a tiny patch three kilometers long. Even so, it is still impressive. On the slopes there are also laurels, maples, strawberry trees, and many others. In spring the Judas tree with its bold blossoms joins the celebration as do other blooms and scents. The trip is worthwhile if only for these.

As mentioned above — up river, En Tamir is still free. The spring pours out from a 30-meter long tunnel. You can go into the tunnel, but there is a "dead spot" on the way and you will have to dive into the unknown. There have been hikers who went in, panicked, and had to be pulled out of the depths by divers. A long tunnel, cold water, and inside perhaps a devil — why be tempted? A good substitute to the tunnel are the tree-ringed pools a few hundred meters from En Tamir. If the winter floods have not completely altered the river it is a good place to bathe, to rest, and to muse over the thought that the Garden of Eden may not have been so bad after all . . . .

Starkenberg or Kal'at Koren — Both Are
MONTFORT

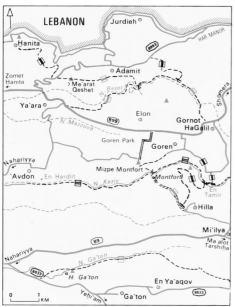

From Nahariyya travel east on Road 89 towards Ma'alot. Between kilometers 15-16 there is a turnoff to Mi'ilya and Hilla. Take the turnoff and drive along the road at the edge of the village and then beyond the village, to the parking area, which is about 4.5 kilometers from the main road. From the carpark it is a 20-30 minute walk to the fortress.

You can come back the same way, but don't forget that the climb up takes longer; or, if you can arrange to be picked up by car at Goren Park, walk down to Nahal Keziv and up to Goren Park.

▲
Inside Montfort Castle

Just as the path ends in the wood, the fortress suddenly appears above. If you look carefully, you can see a channel cut into the hillside near the eastern end of the fortress. From this distance the channel's function is easily discernible. It served as a moat, separating the fortress from the mountain range. Alongside the first moat there is another, smaller one, partly blocked with stones that fell from the eastern wall of the castle. The path you will climb up is not the original one, which was at the eastern side of the fortress. You will take the "tourist path" at the western corner. On the way up look for an opening in the wall. This is the sewage outlet; just beyond it is a breach, perhaps the one begun by the last conqueror of the castle, Babars the Mameluke.

The fortress was first built in Roman times. Not much is known about this structure, although it was fully excavated in 1926. As far as our interests are concerned, the story begins when a fortress was built here by the Crusaders in the middle of the twelfth century. It was part of a large estate of which Mi'ilya was the center. The French called the castle Montfort, meaning "strong hill."

The Crusader orders were generally established to care for and to protect pilgrims. In the course of time the orders developed and became military forces that formed the main power of the Crusader Kingdom. One of these was the German order known as "The Order of St. Mary of the Teutons," or briefly, "The Teutons."

This order was primarily supported by the German Empire. When Jerusalem was conquered by Saladdin, the order's base was moved to Acre, and later when the Teutons inherited western Galilee with its castles (Jedin, Mi'ilya, Montfort) they "moved house" to here, bringing with them their archives, their treasury, and all their valuables. The Teutons gave the place a German name — Starkenberg — meaning, like its previous name, "the strong hill." It became a large, majestic castle, dominating a wide area that took in about 50 agricultural villages. But the renovation and expansion did not last long. Some 40 years after it was acquired by the Teutons in 1266, it was besieged by the Muslim-Mameluke commander, Babars.

The first assault was beaten off, but the Muslims did not give up. In 1271 they again besieged the castle. Signs of the siege can perhaps be detected in the breach seen in the wall from the tourist path going up to the castle. After its defeat the castle was destroyed by its conquerors.

Years passed, and again the castle's name was changed. The Arabs called it Kal'at Koren, meaning "the castle on the horn" — the horn of the hill — and the river was called Wadi-el-Koren.

At the fortress there are remains of walls, rooms, a central column remaining from a vaulted hall, a ruined church, a cistern and even a wine-press. At the east of the fortress is the citadel, with a beautiful view over the river.

If you decide to go down to Nahal Keziv, at the end of the path you will find a Crusader bulding stuck to the mountainside over the river. From outside, this two-storey structure does not look impressive, but it is well worth looking inside. It seems to have been a Crusader farmhouse which supplied food to the castle, but it might have been part of the storehouses, or perhaps some kind of workshop. The second storey is well-preserved, with handsome arches. It is whispered that there is a secret passage from this building to the castle above. But where it begins and where it ends — only the whisperers know . . . .

▶ View of Montfort from Goren Park

Replication of the Battle at
ZOMET HASHAYYARA (Convoy Junction)

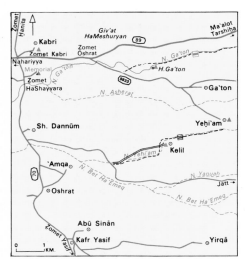

From Nahariyya, drive east on Road 89 in the direction of Galilee. At the crossroads, turn right, and after a few hundred meters left, following the signs.

When the plan to partition Palestine was adopted in November 1947, the settlements of western Galilee — Nahariyya, Elon, Hanita, Mazzuva, and Yehi'am — suddenly found themselves in territory designated to be the Arab State. All of western Galilee was cut off from the Jewish settlement in Haifa and the suburbs, and they were cut off from each other as well. Yehi'am, for example, was isolated in the hills east of Nahariyya, with a number of Arab villages commanding the only road to it.

When the situation of the settlements of western Galilee deteriorated, it was decided to break through to them and bring a convoy of supplies. On March 26, 1948, armored cars set out from Nahariyya for Yehi'am, under the command of Ben-Ami Pechter. Up to about Kabri, the convoy advanced — accompanied by a suspicious silence. The road began to curve, with thick vegetation on either side — an ideal place for an ambush (today the vegetation has disappeared and passage seems simpler). At one of the bends, near the village of Kabri, the road was blocked. As the convoy approached shots were fired at it from all sides. The ambush force, led by the Arab commander, Adiv Shishakli, numbered some 500 men. Facing them were seven armored cars carrying supplies to Yehi'am, headed by a vehicle especially adapted for breaking through roadblocks. On reaching a barrier the vehicle would lower an iron triangle which rammed the barrier and broke through. The blockade runner managed to break through, firing back at the Arab forces, but the car following it was hit and run off the road. That was also the tale of the third car in the convoy. It became evident that the convoy could not get through to Yehi'am. One car that began to turn back to Nahariyya ran into a second barrier and was also stopped. Hundreds of Arabs gathered round, summoned from the village by the sound of firing. The battle was fought from all the vehicles and only at sunset did some of the fighters manage to retreat on foot to Nahariyya. One reached Yehi'am. At the end of the battle Israeli losses numbered, 47, among them the commander, Ben-Ami Pechter.

The western Galilee settlements were completely cut off. Here and there a ramshackle airplane — one of the various Pipers — tried to airlift supplies but the situation remained critical. In Yehi'am water had to be parachuted to the besieged settlers.

The nightmare ended for the settlements of western Galilee only in the middle of May. On May 13 a convoy set out northwards, intending to break through to the settlements. This operation bore the name of the commander of the Yehi'am Convoy — Ben-Ami. The convoy succeeded in reaching Nahariyya and went on from there with no obstruction to Elon, Hanita, Mazzuva, and Yehi'am.

A monument was set up at the place where the Yehi'am Convoy battle took place. It was planned by an architect from Kibbutz Sa'ar, who took pains to preserve the site as it had been at the time of the battle. The map, the explanations at the entrance, and the burnt cars successfully replicate the atmosphere of that period.

▲
Map of the battle at the replication site

▶ Replication of the Yehi'am Convoy

An Ancient Fortress and a View at
YEHI'AM

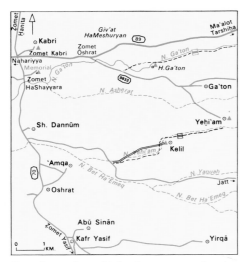

Travel east from Nahariyya on Road 89 in the direction of Galilee. After Zomet Kabri (Kabri Junction) between kilometers 7-8, Road 8833 turns off in the direction of Kibbutz Ga'ton. And before you reach the kibbutz another road will turn towards Yehi'am and the Jedin Fortress.

When the first settlers of the Shomer Hatzair kibbutz movement came to this spot in November, 1946, they made their way by path, took up a position at the fortress, and used parts of its structures. The young settlement was named after Yehiam Weitz, in memory of a member who fell when the Akhziv Bridge was blown up on the "night of the bridges," an operation against the British that preceded the War of Independence.

Establishing the kibbutz was a continuation of the activity begun in the area by the Jewish National Fund in 1938. In Weitz's diary he recorded, "Sixth of April: At the meeting this morning we discussed the question of purchasing in the north. It was unanimously decided to acquire Hirbet Samak (the location of Kibbutz Elon) at the price of 4 Palestinian Pounds per dunam, and Hirbet Jedin, 400 dunams at PP 2.250 per dunam. It was agreed to buy it even though no definite promise had been given by the Jewish Agency to go up there. This is how I described the situation: The lack of a road from the Tarshicha Road, the absence of water, and the scarcity of good land, and in 1939 the price jumped to PP 3 per dunam."

Today the journey is easy and convenient on the road paved by the settlers of Yehi'am. It was not so in the past. A diarist in 1940 described it this way: "We went to Amka, and from there on horseback. At midday we reached the Jedin Fortress. The fortress is in ruins but it stands in a beautiful place and dominates the surroundings. There is no water, only empty cisterns. The soil is hard but some of it can be cultivated, and there is no road . . . ." In the same year, building engineers toured the place in order to examine the possibilities of settlement. Along with the establishment of the kibbutz, it was suggested to turn the fortress into a military training camp.

Yehi'am became a fortress once again when it was cut off from other Jewish settlements at the outbreak of the War of Independence. The story of Yehi'am's isolation and the attempt to reach it is connected with the convoy that was stopped at Kabri. It was not until Operation "Ben-Ami" in May, 1948 that the entire region was liberated, including Yehi'am. Signs of Yehi'am's stand can be seen in positions around the fortress. A narrow path, submerged in vegetation, connects the positions with the fortress.

The Jedin Fortress was built in the Crusader period, probably at the end of the eleventh century or at the beginning of the twelfth, to guard the road from Akko to Turon (today Tibnine) in Lebanon. It began as a small fortress, a link between other fortresses that guarded the road. At the beginning of the thirteenth century the fortress passed over to the Teuton Crusader Order, which owned parks and villages in the area. With the Mameluke conquest at the end of the thirteenth century, Jedin Fortress was apparently destroyed (along with its neighbor Montfort), but its role did not end here. The various conquerors in the region continued to use it. It was thoroughly renovated in the time of the Bedouin ruler Dahar El-Amar, who conquered Galilee in the eighteenth century. Dahar captured the Jedin Fortress from a local ruler by the name of Ahmed El-hasein and, according to one of the descriptions, built in its place "a large fortress with round towers and a moat hewn into the rocks." At the end of Dahar's rule in Galilee the fortress was abandoned and served partly, perhaps, to house peasants who worked in the surrounding area.

After being restored by the National Parks Authority it became one of the most popular sites in the region.

▲
Jedin Fortress at Yehi'am

▶ Yehi'am Fortress and Kibbutz Yehi'am

Water to Akko (Acre) through the
AQUEDUCT

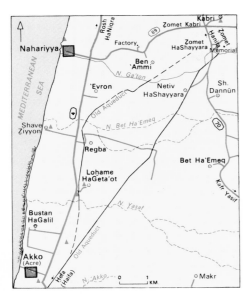

Beautiful sections of the aqueduct are visible from Road 4, which is the Akko (Acre)–Nahariyya Road. Leave your car and take a closer look at several points between kilometers 235-236. One of the most convenient places to stop is the carpark beside the Lohame-HaGeta'ot (Ghetto Fighters) Museum at Kibbutz Lohame-HaGeta'ot.

▲
A section of the aqueduct and the Lohame HaGeta'ot Museum

Israeli old-timers certainly remember the Kabri waters. A resourceful English company filled bottles with water from the Kabri Spring and sold it as superior drinking water to connoisseurs and to those who were not exactly short of cash . . . . But there were some who anticipated the English. These forerunners did not use bottles. They exploited the changes in height at the gushing springs and sent them in aqueducts to a large customer, 12 kilometers from Kabri — the town of Akko! When I looked for a bottle, a memento of the Kabri water, or at least a photograph — I couldn't find anything. But of the acqueduct a substantial remnant has survived.

The earliest aqueduct in this area is over 2,000 years old, and brought water through a tunnel which ran underground for most of its length. Near Kibbutz Lohame-HaGeta'ot, parts of a tunnel and shafts were found. Earthenware lamps characteristic of the Hellenistic period were found in one of the sections, and this is proof that then at least there was an aqueduct here! In the fields in the area there are other fragments, but two aqueducts stand out particularly — the eastern one, whose construction is attributed to the period of a governor named Ahmed Jizzar Facha, and the western one (the one seen clearly from the Akko-Nahariyya Road), built by Suleiman Facha.

Ahmed Jizzar Facha is a well-known figure in the history of Akko — a cruel and despotic governor, but a builder and town renovator. His deeds apparently included the building of the aqueduct from Kabri to Akko. This aqueduct is also marked on the Jaquotin map used during Napoleon's siege of Akko in 1789. The French, who besieged the town, seem to have destroyed the aqueduct, either to reduce the town's water supply or to use the water for their own purposes. A short time after Napoleon's retreat from Akko and from the country a new aqueduct was opened by Suleiman Facha, one of Jizzar's heirs. This aqueduct used the waters of Ein Basha (En Hashayyara) — one of the springs of Kabri — and stretched for over 13 kilometers to Akko. Most of the course of the aqueduct was in a closed channel, and near Akko the two aqueducts — what remained of the aqueduct of Jizzar and the new aqueduct of Suleiman — apparently joined. Although the aqueduct was designed to bring water to Akko it was also used by other clients. In one of the sections, water was drawn off to irrigate the private lands of the governor; sometimes the aqueduct was broken into and water was stolen.

The local residents drew little benefit from the flowing water — save for exceptional events such as a famine or when the aqueduct was being cleaned. Then they could buy the water or steal it when the guards were lax. The aqueduct was operative until the War of Independence and then it was blocked — as it had been by Napoleon — in order to put pressure on the people of Akko. After Israel was established efforts were made to renew the aqueduct's operation, but it was not in good condition. Later it was damaged by floods and the ravages of time gnawed at it. It's a great pity.

There are some really beautiful sections of the aqueduct — some original, some repaired and reinforced. In places where the course passed over a river, bridges were built to support the aqueduct, and these are picturesque. One such bridge may be seen over Nahal Yasaf to the west of Kibbutz Lohame-HaGeta'ot. If you walk south from the carpark alongside the aqueduct you will reach the bridge. In good weather the ridges of Galilee can be seen through the arches of the aqueduct and "the view from the bridge" is very romantic . . . .

▶ The aqueduct from Kabri to Akko near Kibbutz Lohame HaGeta'ot

LOWER GALILEE, AND THE AKKO, KINNAROT, YIZRE'EL AND BET SHE'AN VALLEYS

Lower Galilee is topographically different from its big brother in the north, with peaks rising only half the height of those in Upper Galilee. A number of valleys, permit easy movement from west to east and it is easier to travel than Upper Galilee. The boundary dividing the "brothers" is Bet Keren valley in the north and Nahal Ammud and its streams in the east, and has been defined simply as the road between Akko and Zefat or the new road between Akko and Ammi'ad. Our forefathers made the borderline at Galilean Be'er Sheva, or the nearby Kefar Hananya, and demarcated it: "Wherever sycamores do not grow from Kefar Hananya and above is Upper Galilee. Wherever sycamores grow from Kefar Hananya and below is Lower Galilee." There is much less rain here than in the north and for this reason also less natural woodland on the slopes, although there are still remains of oak forests. Its observation posts can compete with those on higher mountains: The views from Mount Tabor, Givat Hamoreh, or Mount Tur'an are definitely something to behold!

To the west, Lower Galilee is bounded by the Zevulun and Akko Valleys. Once there were many swamps here; today there are settlements and industrial zones, and among all these the Na'aman Nature Reserve.

To the east is Biq'at Kinnarot. Each of the shores of the Kinneret (Sea of Galilee) has its own character — the Jordan River, which enters from the north and emerges from the south of the lake and round about are other streams. Each of the streams is unique: Nahal Ammud, for example, or biqat Beteicha, with many streams flowing and forming lagoons, holy places to Christianity, remains of ancient synagogues, settlements, and of course bathing beaches. Until before the Six Day War the entire lake was Isreali territory, but only in theory. The border was set at ten meters from the waterline all around. Now, on Sabbath and festivals more than ten meters of shore are occupied by holidaymakers . . .

South of the Sea of Galilee are Geon Hayarden and Kikar Hayarden and the mouth of the Yarmouk River and the Jordan Valley. To the south of Lower Galilee are the valleys, among them Yizre'el Valley, and to the east the Harod Valley. From here it is possible to slide down to the Bet She'an Valley and the town of Bet She'an. Rising above all these is Mount Gilboa — but now we have crossed over into Samaria.

A Swamp Reserve at
AFEQ

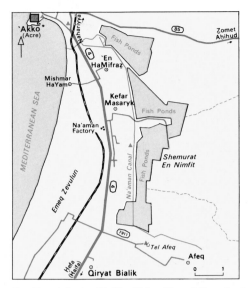

On Road 4, the Haifa-Akko (Acre) Road, between kilometers 222-223, turn in the direction of Kibbutz Afeq and the nature reserve. The entrance to the reserve is about one and a half kilometers from the main road.

There are those who say that when Nahal Na'aman reaches the walls of Akko the foundations of the world will tremble. Still others associate positive phenomena with this meeting. But just to be sure . . . for many years everything was done to prevent the waters of the Na'aman from approaching the town: Water was diverted from the spring, pumped out of the river, and even enclosed in a canal. Anyone who tries today to find the traces of the Na'aman will discover that its upper streams — *wadis* that get to see water only in winter — are Nahal Hilazon, which leaves its mark on northern Lower Galilee, and Nahal Avelim, which comes from Biqat Bet Netufa. But in its springs gushing out around Tel Afeq, where it was almost perennially a river, it is merely . . . a channel. On the main road approaching Akko, near the bridge, it is again "almost a river," a small consolation for fishermen who try their luck there.

In recent years the river has undergone rejuvenation. Veteran students of nature and explorers remembered the Na'aman swamps with nostalgia. A boat trip through something resembling a jungle, a rich world of flora and fauna, was apparently a great experience for adventure lovers. It was almost like a trip through the Hula Swamps. In fact, the swamps extended throughout the Akko Valley. The Bedouins who lived here wove baskets and rugs, raised water buffalo, and suffered from malaria. That was in the past. Then the swamps were drained, and following the pumping operations and development of the water sources there was hardly anything left of the river. The Nature Reserves Authority, the Jewish National Fund, and the township of Qiryat Bialik joined together to restore the site, including Tel Afeq, an ancient flour mill, marsh plants, a hiking path, and parking facilities.

At the entrance is the archaeological mound, Tel Afeq, perhaps the Canaanite Afeq that was situated in the lands of the Tribe of Asher. From the hillock there is a view over the reserve and the entire region.

From here go on to the flour mill. The foundations of the structure are ancient and it is possible that a flour mill operated here even in Roman times. Beside it there is a dam, situated near the building, which was designed to raise the level of the spring water that was directed into sloping channels through which the water fell onto water wheels. These were turned by the force of the water striking blades or wings and turned mill-stones. The large structure was built in the Crusader period and also served as a fortification. At that time the place was called Kurdani, a name that has been preserved, and to this day many of the people call the region and the installations in it Kurdani.

The structure was destroyed during the conquest of Palestine by the Crusaders, but it was restored. The mills were operative here until after World War I, and their clients included the Turkish army. On the ground floor of the mill there is a sound and light show. Just above the Crusader fortification is a fortification built at the time of the 1936 riots. In this structure, there is a memorial room dedicated to sons of Qiryat Bialik who fell in Israel's wars.

From the building there is a path that goes around the reserve and the ancient dam and then returns to the starting point. The dominant landscape is of tamarisks with a tall eucalyptus here and there. The list of river flora and the wildlife in the reserve is long and appears in the leaflet that can be obtained at the entrance to the site.

▲
The dam at Afeq swamp reserve

▶ The fortified mill-house at the Afeq swamp reserve

Over Twenty Strata at
TEL MEGIDDO

At Zomet Megiddo, the junction of Roads 65 and 66, travel a short distance on Road 66 and between kilometers 20-21 turn off to Tel Megiddo.

Megiddo is one of the few places in the world where you can see a 5,000-year-old temple. The round structure seen in the picture was unearthed during the Megiddo excavations. It is an altar eight meters in diameter and about one meter eighty in height, and it is reached by climbing some steps. Several other altars were built beside this one in later periods. In the temple square is the temple to which the altar belongs, and two more temples, one of which contains the bases of two columns which apparently supported the roof.

But the story of Megiddo is not only the story of temples. It is one of the largest tels, or archaeological mounds, in Israel and for this reason it was called Tel El-Mutasallim — the Governor's Hill.

People began to live here about 6,000 years ago, but the city ceased to exist after the Persian rule 2,300 years ago. During its 4,000-year existence towns were built here, one on top of the ruins of another, creating an expansive network of history.

Megiddo is mentioned in many Egyptian documents. One famous description tells of the journey of Thutmose III, his advance to the site, and its conquest. From the list of booty it is possible to imagine the resources of the area 3,500 years ago: 1,929 head of cattle, 2,000 goats, 20,500 sheep, 204 horses, 191 colts, 6 war-horses, 2 fine gold-plated carriages (that had belonged to governors defeated in battle), 30 carriages that had belonged to the allies, 892 carriages of the scattered army . . . and in addition to this, handsome battle armor and 200 army uniforms, 502 bows, and more and more . . . .

The town was conquered by the Hebrews apparently only in the time of King David. King Solomon fortified it and in the days of Ahab, Megiddo became the city where the war-carriages were kept. King Josiah fell near here attempting to fight Pharaoh Necho, and so on and so forth. According to Christian tradition based on the New Testament, the Battle of the End of Days will be fought on the "Hill of Megiddon" — which is Armageddon.

The structures that serve as a museum and the offices of the site were put up by an expedition from the University of Chicago. In the small museum there are photographs of some of the finds, and among them a sacrificial altar from the Israelite period. Important for tourists is a model of the site, which shows different levels of settlement.

The ascent to the actual site brings you first to ancient gates and a substantial remnant from the eastern wing of the gate of Solomon, built much like the gates of the twin towns of that period — Gezer and Hazor. From here, go on to the east of the mound to the observation platform over the valley and to the archaeological section cut in the mound and to the temple square. In the center of the mound are the remains of a large palace with hard-to-distinguish outlines. Beside it is a large, deep pit with two sets of steps. Some 2,700 years ago it served as a granary. There is a great deal written about the stables of Megiddo but all that remains on the spot are posts with holes in them, apparently for tying horses, and stone troughs.

The most impressive site at Megiddo is the ancient water tunnel. The main fact about it is that it gave the city access to water from the spring outside the walls during siege. It was hidden from enemy eyes. From the top of the mound a shaft was dug and within the shaft a staircase led to a tunnel that reached the water. The tunnel is about seven meters long and three meters high. It was cut on a slope in order to let the water flow beneath the shaft and from there it was pumped up. The water system is 2,900 years old and is an amazingly precise engineering feat. A visit is an experience not to be missed.

The water tunnel at Tel Megiddo

▶ The altar in "Temple Square" at Megiddo

A Hidden Landscape at
NAHAL QINI

On Road 66, halfway between Zomet Megiddo (Megiddo Junction) and Tel Megiddo, near a bridge, there is a turnoff onto a dirt road. Drive along it for about one kilometer, turn left onto a cobbled road, and then go down towards the riverbed and the remains of an ancient bridge over Nahal Qini.

If you come in spring, when the blossoms are a riot of color, you will probably go wild too . . . . It is hard to believe that all this magnificence is so near the road, so unknown, and still so clean (except, of course, for cow dung, because cows walk around here as though they own the place). There are flowers and trees — eucalyptus and huge poplars. There is a broken-down *khan,* or Turkish inn, something that was once a flourmill, a road, a river, and a medley of names.

Here are the names, for example: Zomet Megiddo, the junction, was once Zomet Lagun, named for the nearby Arab village. The river is Nahal Qini. There once was a Jewish settlement here called Otnay. And to the north of the river is Giv'at Yoshiyyahu, the Hill of Josiah . . . . A legend tells that our forefather Abraham prayed here near Lagun on his way to Egypt, and even struck the rock with his stick and water came out. And thanks to his stick water now flows in the stream.

Tel Megiddo and its Arabic name Tel El-Mutasallim are discussed on the previous page. Yoshiyhahhu of Giv'at Yoshiyyahu is of course King Josiah, who tried to stop Pharaoh Nacho here and was defeated. The matter of the name Lagun is interesting — just after the Bar Kokheva revolt, the Sixth Roman Legion, the "Iron Legion," was stationed here, and the place was called by its name, Legio, a short name that later grew into the long and dignified title, Maximianopolis, and if *polis* means town, then this is the town of Maximianus, the Roman emperor. The Arabs stuck to the name Lagun, thus preserving the name of Legio. Now Megiddo has returned as the name of the kibbutz next to the tel.

And I almost forgot — Nahal Qini, perhaps named after the river mentioned in ancient sources. Perhaps the Qini tribe lived here (remember Madam Yael, wife of Hever the Qini, who, while fulfilling the duty of hospitality, hammered a tent peg into Sisera's head? For further details, see Judges 4).

Remains of all the events related here barely exist but look for them while touring the place anyway. Begin your tour near the old bridge. From here you can go down or up the river course. Go up and you will pass a forest of eucalyptus trees and then poplars. They are surprisingly tall and strong. After a short walk go down to the remains of a flourmill. While crossing the river you will see a fallen post, and by the mill a fig tree in the stream. It is a beautiful spot. On a hillock rising just above are the remains of the *khan* which served travelers at this important crossroads.

Go along the river course to a dam and a small lake, and then turn on the dirt road near the remains of the Arab village of Legion and its graveyard. Try to return via the old bridge on the other side of the river. It is a miniature jungle and to get lost in it is a real pleasure . . . .

▲
The old bridge at Nahal Qini

▶ Blossom time at Nahal Qini

The Race to Be Buried at
BET SHE'ARIM

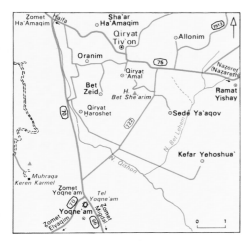

This site can be reached from Qiryat Tiv'on through Qiryat Amal, or simply and easily by traveling east of Qiryat Amal on Road 722, which connects Roads 75 and 70. Between kilometers 4-5 turn west in the direction of the signs to the site.

In the third century, C.E., Bet She'arim was the seat of the Sanhedrin which functioned as supreme court and legislature. But Bet She'arim's main development began when it became . . . a cemetery. After Rabbi Yehuda Hanassi, the head of the Sanhedrin, was buried here, Bet She'arim became much sought after as an eternal resting place. Jews from Israel and the diaspora went to great lengths in order to be laid to rest near the Rabbi, and there are inscriptions etched here in a variety of languages, both burial vaults and coffins, decorated in accordance with the importance of the person and his family's pocket. There are also various engraved pictures, some from Greek mythology, reliefs of lamps, ornamented stone doors, arches, and so on.

The road to the burial vaults is near the remains of an ancient settlement, with structures that include a public building and a ruined synagogue. Just next to the road is an oil press. Bet She'arim was first settled in the Persian and Hellenistic periods, but its main development came after the destruction of Jerusalem. At that time many refugees came to Galilee from Judea and Samaria. When Rabbi Yehuda Hanassi moved the Sanhedrin from Shfaram to Bet She'arim, it became a major center. When Rabbi Yehuda Hanassi was buried here, according to tradition, it became an attraction to the Jews of the diaspora as well. The town was destroyed in 351 C.E., when Gallus Caesar suppressed a Jewish revolt and burnt and destroyed this and other Jewish towns in the region.

Above the area of the antiquities is the house of the Zaid family. Alexander Zaid, a veteran member of the "Hashomer" organization, settled here with his family in 1926 in order to guard the Jewish National Fund forest and its lands. He was killed in 1938 and the statue of a horseman looking out over the valley was erected in his memory. A path branching off from the road going down to the burial vaults leads to the statue.

Many burial vaults are scattered to the west and to the north on the slopes of the Bet She'arim hills. To the west are highly decorated burial vaults built on several levels. The largest and most important vaults are on the northern slope. There are many beautiful and interesting caves, such as the one in the photograph opposite. It is possible to visit some of them, including numbers 14 and 20. Vault number 14 is said to be the burial place of Rabbi Yehuda Hanassi. His name has not been found there, but on the walls of the room inscriptions were found mentioning Rabbi Shimon, Rabbi Gamliel, and Rabbi Anina (Hanina) and perhaps this was the family vault of the Prince's household. The entrance to this vault is very impressive, consisting of three decorated arches and stone doors in imitation of wood.

Vault number 20 is the richest of the vaults and has scores of limestone and marble coffins. The coffins are decorated with Hebrew inscriptions (most of the inscriptions at Bet She'arim are Greek) and many embellishments. There are figures of lions facing each other, a lion chasing its prey, birds, and even a pagan design such as the battle of the Amazons.

One of the caves has been turned into a museum with photographs and finds which complete the picture. And finally — there are those who say that a visit here may also be beneficial. In the Arab village that once stood here, a saint, Sheikh Abrik, was buried who, according to legend, performed a miracle: He made water bubble from a broken jug. This bubbling water created a swamp which cured anyone who bathed in it.

▲
The statue of Alexander Zaid

► A "simple" burial vault at Bet She'arim

Is the Navel of Israel Really at
HAR TAVOR (Mount Tabor)

Drive on Road 65, the Afula–Zomet Golani (Junction) Road. A few kilometers before Kefar Tavor, between kilometers 56-57, turn onto road 7266. Drive past the Arab village of Dabburiya and enter the carpark. From here a narrow road goes up to the peak of Mount Tabor. Ascent on this winding road is permitted only to small vehicles. You can go up on foot along the path and come down the same way, or you can slide down the north-eastern slope of the hill towards the Bedouin village of Arab E-Shibli and come out on Road 65.

You can't miss the Tabor, which is higher than anything around (588 meters above sea level). Long ago in geological time, a mound appeared here as a result of internal pressures. The rising of the mound disturbed mother earth and jets of basalt gushed out. These can be seen at the foot of the mountain and on the way to it. Because of the way it was formed, scientists call this mound a "raised pile." To us it is simply Mount Tabor.

Mount Tabor is also steeped in history. It dominates and commands an important road in the Yizre'el Valley, a section of the historical Via Maris, the coastal road, and it was, therefore, coveted in many periods. It was the meeting point of three tribes: Issaschar, Zevulun, and Naphtali, and when Deborah and Barak battled against the Canaanites the Tabor served as their assembly point for the attack on Sisera's army.

The Tabor knew many other wars. Josephus fortified the peak in an effort to secure the Galilee against the Romans. In the battle that later took place the Romans tricked the Jews: When their drinking water ran out the Roman Commander promised the Jewish fighters that if they surrendered they would not be hurt. When they surrendered he had them all killed.

The mountain was also the site of wars in Crusader times. It was fortified and a church was built on its summit, but like other places of that period it was conquered and destroyed by the Mamelukes.

But the Tabor is not only connected with wars. In the Second Temple period, for example, beacons were lit at its summit to announce the start of the new month.

The Tabor also occupies an important place in Christian tradition. The New Testament tells that Jesus came here with his disciples "and in their presence he was transfigured, his face shone like the sun and his clothes became white as the light. And lo they saw Moses and Elijah conversing with him." This is the ceremony of the transfiguration and the hill is called "the Hill of the Transfiguration" by Christians. This tradition brought Christian pilgrims here as early as the fourth century, and over the course of time monasteries, inns, and other structures were built. These were destroyed by the Mamelukes, but renewal began when the Christians returned to the mountain in the nineteenth century.

When you reach the top of the mountain turn left and follow the road towards a little church maintained by the Greeks. This church is named after Elijah and is built on ancient foundations. Nearby are walls and a tower from the mountain fortifications. Go back to the head of the road the way you came. Wander around near the gate and walk a bit in the moat at its south, turning right at the ditch until you get to a quarry and a cave; or just walk in the moat and in the wood, or try encircling the hill by the moat. The path is pleasant and it will bring you to the east of the church, to an area held by the Franciscan Church. To the right of the road is a hostel for pilgrims, a clock tower, and next to the carpark a small local museum. To the left of the carpark is sundial and beside it antiquities. The impressive structure is the church, which was built about 60 years ago. At the front of the two towers are chapels in honor of Moses and Elijah! Inside, there are remains of ancient synagogues, mosaics, and additional rooms.

Finally, go up on one of the roofs (to the right of the towers) to the observation post and look out at other views. Some explorers connect the name Tabor with the word navel (Tabur in Hebrew) — and if we are really at the center of Israel then there are surely many landscapes around us....

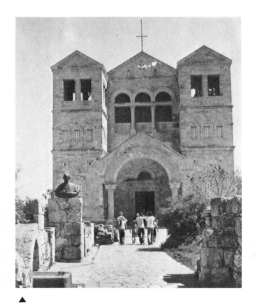

The Franciscan Church on Mount Tabor

▶ Mount Tabor

A Beautiful View from the Castle at
KOKHAV HAYARDEN (Belvoir)

Road 717 branches off from the Emeq Road west of En Harod, between kilometers 28-29. This road leads to the settlements Ramat Zevi and Moledet. The entrance an Kokhav Hayarden is between kilometers 16-17.
Visit here in the late afternoon when the light is at your back. You can then continue on down Road 717 to the Jordan Valley.

▲
The eastern gate of the fortress

Belvoir is not only a Crusader castle but as its name indicates, it has a beautiful view, as well. Centuries ago, a Muslim commander who tried to capture it from the Crusaders described it as "joining the stars, an eagle's nest, and the habitation of the moon." And that's how it looks from below. When you reach it from the west and from the carpark you will be on the same level as the fortress.

In order to cut it off and separate it from its surroundings a deep moat was hewn around it, whose main purpose was to prevent battering rams from breaking down the walls.

The entrance to the fortress is over a new wooden bridge to the western gate. Entrance is through the outer fortification which surrounds the entire fortress; domes and walls can still be seen. Once inside, cross the courtyard surrounding the central core of the tower — the Citadel — which has two storeys, a square yard, and four turrets. The dining hall and the kitchen were located in the courtyard. The water cistern was also there, under arches. The church was on the second storey. Several decorated stones, one with a design of a seven-branched candelabrum, can be discerned on the walls of the fortress. These apparently belonged to an ancient synagogue from a place called Kokhav that was situated on a hillock near the fortress.

Leave the fortress from the east side, and from there look towards the Jordan, across the Jordan, and to Biq'at Kinnarot. The location of the fortress and the broad view from it explain its importance. It was acquired by the Hospitaller Order and, according to the price paid for it, it was apparently a small castle which was enlarged and fortified by the members of the Order. Its position above the valley and overlooking important roads, and its proximity to the border of the Jerusalem Crusader Kingdom of that time made it a spot of great importance. Most of the stories connected with the fortress deal with its stand against Saladdin's army. After the defeat of the Crusaders in 1187, in the battle of the Horns of Hittin, almost the entire kingdom fell into the hands of the Moslims. Tyre and Belvoir remained after Zefat, Tibnine, and Kal'at Shakif, the last three citadels, had fallen. Now a vast army was sent to conquer the fortress. For 18 months they besieged it. Winter made the siege difficult and the Crusaders' sallies exhausted the besiegers. Saladdin himself was summoned. The Moslims dug a trench beneath the south-eastern tower and managed to topple part of the tower, but the citadel remained intact. Finally the residents of the castle surrendered and were allowed to be evacuated to Tyre. A few years later the castle was destroyed so that it could not be used again as a fortress.

In the eighteenth century, Bedouins settled near the fortress and built a meager village named Kawkab El-Hawa, meaning star of the winds. In 1948, an Iraqi militia force crossed the Jordan, attacked Kibbutz Gesher, and one unit moved towards the castle, intending to take up positions there. Israeli forces anticipated the enemy by one day and greeted them with a barrage of fire. Two 65 mm. cannons — the "Napoleonchiks" — that had shelled the Iraqis next to Gesher, were brought up here. A cannon like this is exhibited in the Tiberias town square, and the local comedians say that the biggest revolver they have ever seen is on display in Tiberias . . . .

▶ Kokhav Hayarden and the Jordan Valley

The Story of a Messiah at
ARBEL

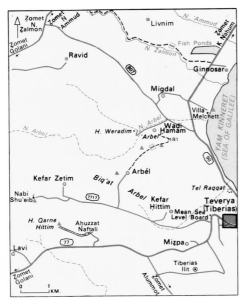

Take Road 77 from Zomet Golani (Junction) in the direction of Teverya (Tiberias). Just before Teverya, between kilometers 78-79, there is a turnoff to Road 7717, to Biq'at Arbel. Follow the signs to Moshav Arbel, look for the remains of a synagogue, and then follow the road to the observation post, which is at an altitude of 181 meters above sea level.

▲
A view from the cliffs at Arbel

Drive slowly on the road to Biq'at Arbel. After all, one of the traditions connected with the place is that a Messiah, Menachem Ben-Amiel, will appear here and meet the Prophet Elijah and the sages of Israel. There is a hint at this tradition in the Jerusalem Talmud: "Once a farmer was ploughing his field at Biq'at Arbel. Suddenly his ox brayed. A passing Arab heard the braying and said: 'Jew! Jew! Untie your ox and untie your plough because the Temple is destroyed!' After some time the ox brayed again. The same Arab said: 'Jew! Jew! Tie up your ox and tie up your plough because Messiah the King is born!' The Jew said: 'What is his name?' The Arab replied: 'Menachem . . . from the king's capital of Judean Bethlehem.'"

On the road you will pass Kefar Hittim, where Jews tried to work the land in the nineteenth century. Rabbi Haim Eliezer Waks relates that in 1876 he bought "three groves in Kefar Hittin and planted hundreds of citron trees. Ten years later the newspaper, *Hamelitz,* tells of 13,000 citron trees on Eliezer Waks' estate. Despite this auspicious beginning, Kefar Hittim was not lucky. At the beginning of this century the Jewish National Fund acquired lands in the area and various settlers tried to gain a foothold, but without success. It was abandoned several times. In 1914 a group of six workers known as the Lodz Group came here. In 1924 religious settlers established Moshav Hittin. And in 1937 the permanent settlement was established: the *Kotzer* organization set up the cooperative settlement of Kefar Hittin.

Go past Kefar Hittim and turn towards Moshav Arbel. You will be near the edge of the old settlement. After the destruction of the Second Temple Joshua's guards, the priestly custodians, were stationed here, among them Nitai the Arbelite, who was Head of the High Court in the Tanaitic period.

The remains of the synagogue here were mentioned by travelers many years ago. Shmuel Ben-Shimshon wrote in 1210: "And we went up to Arbel and there is the big synagogue built by Nitai the Arbelite." At one point the graves of Jacob's children, Dina, Levi, and Shimon, were said to be located beside the synagogue. Adam's son Seth was also said to be buried here. Shmuel Ben-Shimshon refers to this: "And near to Arbel are three tribes of the sons of Jacob and Dina their sister and beside the flock grows a beautiful myrtle and none may take a branch from it, neither a Jew nor Ishmaelite, for fear of punishment. And near there is another sage. And the water pipe passes over it and it is covered with earth and the water falls in the spring in a kind of pit. And they say this is Seth, son of the first man."

Walk around among the ruins of the settlement. You will come across pillars that reveal the location of the synagogue. Whereas synagogue entrances were generally set to face Jerusalem, the synagogue at Arbel is exceptional in this respect. Its entrance is set in the eastern wall, while there is a recess in the southern wall that faces Jerusalem. Explorers with the British Palestine Exploration Fund in the nineteenth century thought that this recess was part of a mosque that was built over the synagogue. Today, it is understood that there were several stages of building and in one of the stages a permanent place was arranged for the Holy Ark, in an alcove facing Jerusalem.

The cliffs seen from the synagogue encircle the Arbel River. They contain caves and the remains of structures and are an interesting tour in themselves.

▶ The remains of the ancient synagogue at Arbel

A Pillar of Rock at
LOWER NAHAL AMMUD (Lower Ammud River)

Between kilometers 425-426 Road 90, along the west coast of Yam Kinneret (the Sea of Galilee), branches off to Road 8077, in the direction of Kibbutz Huqoq. Between kilometers 2-3 the road passes over Nahal Ammud. Park at the side of the road, go down to the river, and walk up its course on the path marked in black ▆. About half a kilometer up river you will see the Ammud, which is Hebrew for pillar, the Ammud spring (if it is bubbling), and if you continue for another one and one half kilometers, the "siphon."

▲
Water in upper Nahal Ammud

It is difficult to decide which system is better — the one used by the Arabs, who call every part of a river by a different name, generally a name characteristic of it, or the system that gives one name to the whole length of a river. But will a single name really reduce confusion?

For example, Nahal Ammud is 25 kilometers long and is called Ammud from its head to where it pours into the Sea of Galilee. Today, when we say Nahal Ammud we picture the orchards, the pools, and the fruit which are to be found in an upper section of Nahal Ammud. The Arabs used to call this section Wadi Tawahin, because of the many flourmills, and even Wadi Tufah, Arabic for apple, because apples and many other fruits characterize the upper part of the river (so we heard once from a shepherd we met here). The name Wadi Ammud, therefore, referred only to the lower part of the river, from the famous pillar of rock that appears in the photograph, and En Ammud beside it, down to the Kinneret (the Sea of Galilee).

And so, to avoid error: In the section described here there are no fruit and no pools. There are, on the other hand, caves, cliffs, a beautiful rock pillar, and perhaps a bit of water. And with a little effort — also the story of the National Water Carrier, the "siphon."

First, regarding the prehistoric caves: Some 400 meters down from the bridge there is Me'arat A-Zotea, the Cave of the Skull, and further on Me'arat Amira, Amira Cave. These two caves are famous in the prehistory of the country. Amira Cave was unearthed in 1925, revealing important prehistoric finds. In the Cave of the Skull, near to the road, tools were found, and more important, a broken skull which was later called Paleantropus Palestinensis, that is, Israelite man — our own early Neanderthal man. But there are also caves where prehistoric remains were found near the pillar itself.

The pillar that gave the entire river its name was once part of the cliff beside it. Perhaps stones have feelings and the pillar wanted to be alone . . . . One way or another, the rock surrounding it eroded and became a sign indicating where the cliff once touched this section. Near the pillar is Ammud Cave. This was uncovered by Japanese archaeologists some 20 years ago and here another skeleton of Paleantropus Palestinensis along with many of his tools was found.

North of the pillar is the entrance to the canyon. Apparently this was the section referred to by the explorer Tristram when he visited here in 1846 and wrote that this was a narrow gorge between lime escarpments, about 150-200 meters high, that the place was always shaded and that the rock walls were so close that his party sometimes had to ride with the current in the river. Of the pillar he wrote: "From inside the gorge in the middle, a single high pillar rises up, inhabited by vultures on all sides."

About 600 meters to the north there is another cave that revealed prehistoric finds, and beyond it up the river, the huge siphon. This is part of the National Water Carrier which flows as an open channel. In a number of streams siphons were built to help move the water from one end to the other. The siphon acts on the principle of connected vessels: The water goes down to the closed pipe from a high point at the east of the river, and comes up again at its west to continue in the open channel. The work here met with difficulties because of the cliff and although today it might seem like a simple diagonal concrete surface, it is really very impressive.

▶ The pillar at Nahal Ammud

A Tunnel from the Nile in Egypt to
EN SHEVA (Heptapegon)

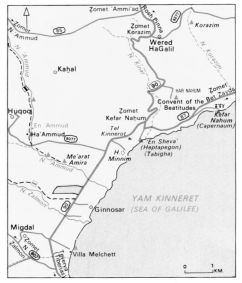

Turn off the Teverya (Tiberias)–
Rosh Pinna Road, Road 90, at Zomet
Kefar Nahum (Junction) onto Road 87.
After a few hundred meters you will be at
the entrance to the site.

Nahal Kinar and its tributaries brought silt here from the hills of Galilee. The silt, the live springs, and the heat made the little valley north-west of the Kinneret (Sea of Galilee) into a fertile area, very hospitable to human settlement. In the course of time, Christian traditions became associated with the little valley, making it also a place of pilgrimage.

The Arabic name Tabigha is a distortion of the Greek name, Heptapegon. The Hebrew translation of this is En Sheva, the English, seven springs. Don't try to look for all seven, since the number apparently served as a symbolic concept more than a reality.

The main Christian sites here are connected with stories in the New Testament and with the deeds of Jesus in the neighborhood of the Sea of Galilee. During the period of the Second Temple, the area was densely populated and it was here that Jesus taught his gospel. On Har (Mount) Nahum which rises above the valley, he preached a famous sermon and, according to the New Testament, performed in En Sheva one of his greatest miracles — the miracle of the loaves and fishes. Five thousand of Jesus' followers had gathered to listen to him preach, after which he fed them all with only five loaves of bread and two fishes. An ancient mosaic floor — a relic of an early church — is on the site. It depicts the miracle with a basket of bread and the fish, and contains many decorative elements — water fowl, marsh plants, houses, and other structures, and a drawing of a device that served to measure the height of water. The floor is in the possession of the Benedictine Order. Another smaller church near the water is called Tabula Domini, the "master's table," or St. Peter's. It was here that Jesus appeared after his death and dined with his disciples.

But there are not only Christian sites in the valley. At the eastern edge there is En Iyov or Hammam El-Ayub, that is, Job's Bath. This is a large pool and, according to Arab tradition, Job bathed here and was healed of his sores. Sore sufferers take note. The largest spring is En Nur; its water is hot and sulphuric and comes from an ancient octagonal pool which was repaired by one Ali A-Tahar, the son of the Bedouin governor, Tahar El-Amar, in the eighteenth century, and is sometimes also called by his name. A unique crab, the blind crab, lives in this pool, and nowhere else in the world; it is 100 per cent Israeli.

Water was piped from the pool in a conduit and the height difference was utilized to operate a turbine that served to draw water from the Sea of Galilee. The spring water was also used to power flour mills and even during one period, to generate electricity for the Italian monastery on the top of Har Nahum.

Fish, including the cat fish, were attracted to the warm water of En Nur. The cat fish, a resident of the Sea of Galilee, is also found in Egypt. This led to many hypotheses, including one that maintained that a long tunnel connected the Sea of Galilee with the Nile. Josephus contributed to the story, writing: "And there are some who think this spring to be one of the arteries of the Nile of Egypt because it breeds fish in a form . . . which is found in the Nile near Alexandria."

A segment of the mosaic in the remains of the Church of the Multiplication

▶ En Sheva and the cliffs of the Arbel in the background

A Wealth of Designs Carved in Stone at
KEFAR NAHUM (Capernaum)

Turn off the Teverya (Tiberias)– Rosh Pinna Road, Road 90, at Zomet Kefar Nahum (Junction) onto Road 87 and drive about 3 kilometers to the entrance to the site, which is between kilometers 2-3.

The grass is always greener on the other side of the fence and people always reach for what is just beyond their grasp. Imported merchandise is usually expensive, and although what we have at home is perhaps just as good, it is not appreciated. What is all this about? In Jerusalem, for example, a monument to Theodor Herzl is made of black basalt. In that part of the country, basalt is rare and special. Here, on the other hand, where there is lots of basalt, what is special is of course light limestone . . . . But it is not only the limestone but also size and splendor that made the synagogue at Kefar Nahum the most magnificent of the ancient synagogues in Israel. The synagogue is maintained today by the Franciscans, who have conducted archaeological excavations that have led to a controversy concerning the age of the synagogue.

Kefar Nahum, Capernaum, is mentioned in the New Testament as a place where Jesus taught and also as the home of one of his disciples, the fisherman, Peter. Excavations at the site identified as Capernaum began during the last century and continued into the beginning of this century. The Franciscan Order hoped that through these excavations they would discover the place where Jesus preached. Jesus lived, as we know, at the beginning of the first century. However, the synagogue uncovered in the excavations is similar in structure and decoration to other synagogues in Galilee of the third century C.E., with repairs and renovations from a later date. Excavations around the site revealed residential structures from the settlement that stood here, and to the south of it a mosaic floor was exposed — part of a church from the fifth or sixth century. Here apparently, beneath the later floor, was the house of St. Peter. There had been a Jewish settlement at Kefar Nahum which evidently did not welcome Jesus with enthusiasm. As a result, Capernaum and its neighbors, Bet Zayda and Korazim, were cursed by him in these words: "And as for you, Capernaum, will you be exalted to the skies? No, brought down to the depths! For if the miracles had been performed in Sedom which were performed in you, Sedom would be standing to this day." Later, in the Middle Ages, travellers visited and wrote of the grave of Rabbi Tanhuma, and perhaps the name Kefar Nahum was preserved as a result.

The entrance to the synagogue is through a paved courtyard reached by several steps. In the large hall there were three rows of columns, one column of which has been re-erected. Around the walls are stone benches and the entire area is paved in stone. Inscriptions were found on two of the columns. One, in Aramaic, says: "Halfo son of Zevida, son of Yochanan, made this column, may he be blessed"; and the second — in Greek — tells of the philanthropist who set up the column. The front entrance of the synagogue faced Jerusalem and had three doors. Various agricultural tools are gathered in the synagogue courtyard, and along the way and in the southern part there are decorated stones, including capitals, lintels, and floral designs. An interesting etching is found on a splinter of stone — a structure resembling a temple with columns and a gate borne on a chariot. There are also a seven-branched candelabrum, a ram's horn, and an incense bowl. If you come upon Israeli coins minted between 10 and 20 years ago there is a good chance the designs came from objects found here.

▲

An acanthus whose leaves appear as a decoration in ancient art, in Jewish synagogues, and at Kefar Nahum

▶ The ancient synagogue at Kefar Nahum

Flowing Water and a Flour Mill at
HAYARDEN PARK

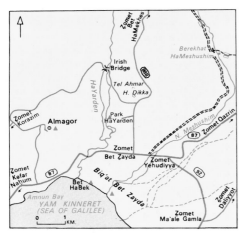

The southern part of Hayarden Park is near the northern shore of Yam Kinneret (The Sea of Galilee) east of the Jordan River. It can be reached by traveling on Road 87, from Zomet Kefar Nahum (Junction) in the direction of the Golan. After traversing the Arik Bridge between kilometers 9-10, turn north onto road 888. Between kilometers 1-2 there is a turn-off to the park. Road 888 can also be reached from Zomet Bet HaMekhes, the old Customs House Junction on Road 91.

Hopefully, ecological disturbances will not ruin what is left of the Jordan and that we will continue to enjoy the stretch from Gesher Benot Ya'aqov (Bridge) to its outflow into Yam Kinneret (the Sea of Galilee). The southern part of the park broadens into the north of Biq'at Bet Zayda or simply into north Betaycha. Roads, carparks, flour mills, and the murmur of flowing water make it a delightful spot.

One can hardly see the archaeological remains here for the trees. The remains are few and are not sufficiently developed to warrant a visit. For example, the town Julias sat on Tel Mashpa. This was the holiday resort of Philippus, son of King Herod. When Philip was nominated as Prince of the Bashan he established his home at Panyas and built his winter home at Julias, in this warm spot, and named it after the daughter of the Roman emperor. Josephus fought the army of Agrippas here over the roads leading from the Golan area and, according to his report, was not victorious here as a result of having fallen with his horse into a swamp.

At the north of the site, at Hirbet Dikka, remains of a synagogue were found. More recently, it was also the site of a Syrian outpost that once threatened Korazim.

Begin your tour from the carpark northwards. Look out from one of the hills to the Jordan River as it is before it enters the park. The river splits into several streams, some of which channel water to the thickly vegetated area that, from here seems impenetrable. Later, go down and walk along paths which lead to charming spots among the running waters and trees on the banks of the Jordan. There are willows, tamarisks, eucalyptus, and even palms and an Atlantic pistachio.

Near the water you can enjoy the raspberry fruit (in season) which grows near the reeds, the cyperuses, and other water plants. In the center of the area stood the village of Talawiya, named after the Bedouin tribe that once lived here. When the park was restored by the Jewish National Fund and its partners, the Nature Reserves Authority and the Kinneret Administration, one of the flour mills that operated here was also restored. In the past the abundant Jordan water worked several flour mills, but many were completely destroyed. The restored mill is a real attraction to tourists. When the mill was in operation, the water came rushing in a conduit to a sloping channel which narrowed at the bottom. When the water was forced through the narrow opening it fell onto a wheel with blades or wings and turned them. Millstones attached to the wheels ground the flour. A grinding day was a holiday for the villagers. True, they stood in line, but the longer the line the greater the number of stories and the longer the discussion of the world's problems.

▲
The mouth of the Jordan seen from Almagor

▶ The flour mill at Hayarden Park

Pleasant Winter Bathing at
HAMMAT GADER

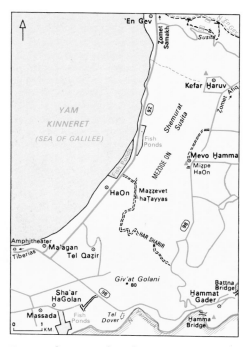

On Road 90, travel to the southern shore of the Sea of Galilee to Tzemach, and along Road 98 to Hammat Gader.

Opinions are divided: Some say it's a little patch of Paradise, and others claim that its dreadful heat is reminiscent of hell. Whichever, our Sages bathed here in ancient times, and today it is an all-year-round resort fit even for alligators . . . .

Let's begin with the Paradise–hell controversy. True, it's hot here in summer. Very. After all, this little valley is situated about 150 meters below sea level. But at least there are pools to bathe in. Paradise refers to the views, the sound of the Yarmouk River flowing at the edge of the site, and of course to the hot springs which are a joy in the cold months. Come in winter and you'll see people in bathing suits, shorts, half-naked — yet minutes from here it is very cold . . . and further north it's even snowing.

This miniature paradise was known to our forefathers, and in the period of the Mishnah, some 1,800 years ago, they came here to bathe; there was even a Jewish settlement here. One of the most famous bathers was Rabbi Yehuda Hanassi, and in his footsteps, of course, came other scholars.

In fact, Hammat Gader was only a "branch" or a suburb of the larger town which stood on the hill above, namely Gader itself. Today its place is taken by a large Arab village named Um-Kis, which is in Jordanian territory. In order to distinguish between this and other places in Israel with similar names, it was called Hammat Gader. The Jews of Gader had problems in their time: Was it, they queried, permitted or forbidden to go down from Gader to Hammat Gader on the Sabbath? Their solution — a compromise: "The rabbi permitted the people of Gader to go down to Hamata and up to Gader but the people of Hamata could not go up to Gader." That's it. It appears that using the Sabbath for bathing is permitted, but going up town for business is not.

There are many remains at the site. At its edges an early Jewish synagogue (fourth or early fifth century) with a mosaic floor was excavated. The floor was taken away but the mound, with remnants of the excavations, has a good view of the Yarmouk, the Yarmouk Bridge, and the other side of the border.

Remains of a Roman theater are also on the site. The area was fenced in and the hill on which it was built today serves as a park with many kinds of animals.

Most outstanding are the remains of the Roman bathhouse. Even before archaeologists began exposing its walls, there were definite hints, such as arches, that something impressive lay beneath . . . . Throughout several recent digging seasons one of the biggest and most impressive ancient bathhouses in the country was uncovered. It contains several rooms and pools, a channel and drainage system, fountains and a majestic entrance, dedicatory inscriptions and even . . . a pool for lepers.

Hammat Gader has several hot springs, four with mineral waters and one with fresh water. The temperature of the spring water ranges between 40 and 52 degrees C. In the period before the establishment of Israel there were also baths at Hammat Gader. Today it is maintained jointly by several Golan Heights kibbutzim. Only part of the complex has been developed. A covered pool has been built and a large swimming pool has been improved. Near this is a fresh-water pool, a small fall, and a "mud pool." In order to attract tourists, alligators were brought here, causing a controversy as to whether this was a suitable place to accommodate them. There were also fears that they would invade the Sea of Galilee and dispossess us . . . . Meanwhile there are about 120 and more alligators of all sizes in pools with passageways and bridges between them.

If you come here to bathe be very careful where you go in. These alligators are not the most pleasant bathing companions!

Alligators in the pools at Hammat Gader — these are young ones and are still playful . . . .

▶ Hammat Gader

"Near the Gate of Paradise —
BET SHE'AN"

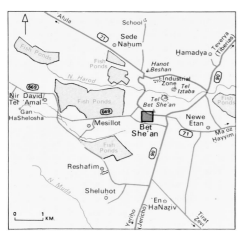

Bet She'an is a junction and can be reached by several roads: Road 90 from the Jordan Valley or Tiberias; Road 669 from Gan Hashelosha; or Road 71 from Afula. The main turnoff into the town is from Road 71, between kilometers 39-40.

Bet She'an became an important town for many reasons. Several roads pass near it, making it a crossroads. It has springs nearby, a hot climate, and good conditions for agriculture. There has been a town here for the past 8,000 years, from the late Stone Age to today.

Bet She'an was visited by the pharaohs of Egypt on their expeditions of conquest. The Philistines, who kept mainly to the south coast of the land of Israel, lived here also. When the town was conquered by Alexander the Great it became known as Scythopolis. The Hasmoneans conquered it, and fought here against the Romans. With the rise of Christianity it also became a religious center. After the Moslim conquest, in the seventh century, the center moved to Tiberias and Bet She'an lost its importance. In the Middle Ages it was a waystation with a *khan,* but through it all it remained a small town. During the War of Independence the town was conquered and abandoned — and then resettled by immigrants after Israel was established.

Begin at the small museum at the edge of the town, which contains a collection of archaeological finds, among them interesting mosaic floors. There is also a map of the town's sites here. Leave the museum in the direction of the bus station and the municipal park. You will pass what was once a Crusader building that borders on the road. Further along the road is the *Saraya* — the Turkish administration building. On the way to the theater you will pass part of the excavated Hippodrome.

Occasionally performances are held at the theater. Entrance is through eight tunnels which admitted an audience of 4,500. Rows of steps divide the space into eight blocks. The theater area was roofed in and square holes show where beams were fixed and where sheets were spread over them for shade. After all, it is very hot in Bet She'an. Beyond the stage is a wall with niches for statues and a passageway, perhaps for the use of stage hands. There are additional entrances for theater employees and an entrance for honored guests.

Opposite the theater, to the north, stands Tel Bet She'an. In most mounds in Israel settlement ceased in the Hellenistic period. Here, the town at the top moved down from the mound and spread; even so the mound remained the center of public and religious life. The mound has been excavated but only a few remains can be seen — part of walls, columns, and a section of road. In the area of Tel Itztaba (near the industrial zone) are additional remains, and the monastery of Kiri Maria — Our Lady Miriam (the key is available at the Bet She'an Museum.) This is a monastery with beautiful mosaic floors.

There is, of course, a Jewish angle at Bet She'an: For many years it was in the hands of foreigners, and the Philistines hung the body of King Saul on its wall after his defeat at Mount Gilboa. In the Hasmonean period the Jews ruled here, and even tried to impose their religion on the foreigners. The Jewish community was diminished here in the great revolt against Rome, but it revived in later periods since the temptation to settle here was strong: Bet She'an was not considered part of the Land of Israel and inhabitants were thus exempt from the obligations of tithes, etc.

And of course, we must mention Eshtori Haparchi who lived here at the end of the Middle Ages. This geographer wrote the book, *Button and Flower,* containing many details on the Palestine of that period. Of Bet She'an he wrote: "I chose to sit here, on this place of many waters, still waters and a blessed land of beauty and full of joy like the garden of the Lord . . . and near the gate of Paradise."

Perhaps, but not in the blazing summer days.

▲
A section of mosaics in the church of Kiri Maria

▶ Theater at Bet She'an

Territories Change Hands at
GEON HAYARDEN

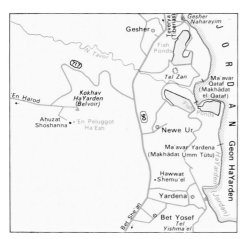

There are several interesting observation posts along the Jordan River whose positions change from time to time (more of this later). Among those recommended: near Kefar Ruppin, around Kibbutz Gesher, and if you chance by on a visit, near the Allenby Bridge (the latter two are south of this map).

▲
The Um-Tzutz–Jordan Ford — one of the Jordan crossings which served as a crossing and a first connection between Jordan and Israel after the Six Day War.

Where can a piece of land pass from Jordan to Israel and back without war, negotiations, diplomatic contacts, or even simple trading? What river's length as the crow flies is half its actual length? The answer to both questions, of course, is the Jordan, Israel's largest river.

There are several rivers in the country and each of them does as it pleases. One flows into the Mediterranean, another spills into the Sea of Galilee. The Jordan is an inland river — its head and sources are at the foot of Mount Hermon and after bathing in the Sea of Galilee it runs to the lowest place in the world, the Dead Sea, where it disappears. Its sources, the Dan, the Hermon (Panyas), the Snir (Hatzbani), and other streams, flow between the Hermon and the Hula Valley. When the Hula Lake was at the height of its power before being drained, it absorbed the streams of the Jordan and moulded them in its melting pot into one river. Several springs entered the Hula Lake from the north and emerged from the south as one — united. It is not far from here to the Sea of Galilee and the Jordan flows between the hills of the Golan and Galilee. From the Sea of Galilee southwards the Jordan's bed determines its form and route. The designer of the river's main bed here was the big lake, the Jordan Lake, which many years ago (in geological terms) stretched from Hatzeba in the south to the Sea of Galilee in the north. Clay deposits known as *Hawar Halashon,* formed on the bed. It is light-colored, brittle matter which sometimes crumbles to the touch. On this soft and pleasant, but unsteady bed the Jordan began to flow between the "northern remnant" of the great lake, the Sea of Galilee, and the "southern remnant," the Dead Sea.

Now picture the flow of the Jordan over this formation. For years the river cut a path which gradually deepened. As the river deepened the cliffs on either side of it grew higher. But since the cliffs were made of *Hawar* they were soft. The higher they rose the less solid they became. As the river bends water seeps under the sides of the cliff. After the base has worn away, a large block of *hawar* falls into the river, and the river quickly adapts to the situation, changes its direction slightly, and again cuts itself a path through the deposits. Imagine the collapse of a mass large enough to block the water for a time. The length of time the Jordan is blocked depends on the size of the *hawar.* It seems that when the Israelites crossed the Jordan on entering the Land of Israel, along with the other miracles the Jordan simply stood as one block thanks to a large block of *hawar* that had collapsed. And this happens today as well. Sometime the river is blocked and after some time forces its way through. Its bends change and a piece of land that was once west of it is now to its east, and vice versa. Once one of the bridges of the Jordan became an orphan because the river deserted it and a piece of land passed from one country to another.

The region of the Jordan's flow is called Geon HaYarden, known to the Arabs as the Zor. The step above it is Kikar HaYarden (the Ghor) which contains most of the settlements that are supplied by Jordan water. The slopes between the Kikar and Geon HaYarden intersect, forming interesting scenery. The most fascinating of all is Geon HaYarden. Once there was thick flora here, but most of the area has now been cultivated; parts of it have been destroyed as a result of border incidents and the building of military roads. Still in parts of Geon HaYarden there are Euphrates poplars and a thick forest of Jordanian tamarisk. Some areas are a veritable maze, with the active help of other plants. From certain spots it is possible to discern deserted streams.

When you look out over the river, pay attention not to cross over with the look-out cliff into neighboring Jordan.

▶ Geon HaYarden

THE CARMEL, CARMEL COAST, SHARON, AND SAMARIA

In geological terms the Carmel is a raised block. In everyday terms the Carmel is the town of Haifa, several Druse villages, and a large nature reserve and park. The mountain, which approaches 500 meters at some of its peaks (497 is its highest), and is near the sea, receives a great deal of rainfall, and therefore has highly developed flora. It has pine forests, several springs, and mountainous landscapes. The suburbs of Haifa threatened to infiltrate parts of the park. These and the planned quarries almost deprived us of a large part of the mountain, but the struggle of the friends of the Carmel and nature lovers prevented the axe from falling. Most of it was declared a nature reserve and a national park, and camping sites were set up, hiking paths were cut, and observation platforms built. Its nearness to crowded population centers is both an advantage and a disadvantage.

At the foot of the Carmel is the Carmel Coast and the Sharon Plain. The shores of the Mediterranean that were not snatched by settlements or hotels are left to us for swimming and sunbathing. The nearness of the beaches to the Carmel and to Samaria permits wonderful summer outings; a dip in the sea and a rest on the hill, or a walk ending in a swim. Although the beach gets more crowded from year to year don't forget that most of Israel's population lives between Tel Aviv and Haifa.

To the east stretches Samaria and the small Samarian desert. Once only old-timers and hikers knew Samaria. Since the Six Day War many others have discovered it, as well. The springs of Samaria, of which there are still plenty, are only some 30 minutes from Tel Aviv and other population centers. One example: Nahal Qana. About the same amount of travelling brings you to an observation point, of which there are also many. An example: Deir Qal'a. And if you want to get to know Samaria by car only you will come across primeval landscapes such as the one on the Hotze-Shomeron (cross-Samaria) Road for example, which, within a short time goes from the coastal plain, across the Samarian hills and desert and then reaches the Jordan. This is a latitudinal cross-section of the country, and contains a wide variety of landscapes in close proximity.

"Little Switzerland" at
NAHAL KELAH (Kelah River)

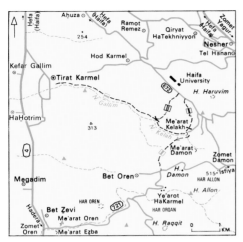

Drive along the Haifa–Isfiya Road, Road 672, and between kilometers 42-43 turn south onto a narrow road that leads to the campsites and a network of paths. At the Mevo Nahal Kelah Campsite there is a path marked in red ▨ which crosses Nahal Kelah towards the Pitulim Campsite near the entrance to Bet Oren on Road 721.

South of Road 672 there is a network of campsites and paths that are part of the development of the Karmel (Carmel) National Park by the National Parks Authority. The road to Nahal Kelah leads to the Mizpor Hatzuk campsite. Walk along the nearby paths till you reach Mizpor Hanof in the direction of Nahal Gallim and the seashore. The view from Miztpor Hatzuk will give you some sense of this section of road, which is about 45 minutes from Nahal Kelah campsite. Or, you can go there directly by car and begin on the path marked in red ▨ . Nahal Kelah begins near Damun jail and flows into Nahal Gallim. Although the objective of this trip are the path and Nahal Kelah, in fact, you will only walk along its banks for a little while before you cross over it and follow a different route. The path will go through wooded cliffs in which the common oak and the terebinth dominate. It is no more than a narrow road in the heart of the nature reserve, but in the past it was the road used by residents of the Carmel who lived on a hill south of Bet Oren.

Once the traffic to Haifa rolled hazardously along here. (In August, 1938, a car carrying watchmen and two women to the Carmel forests was attacked near here. The driver was wounded and the watchmen, after a long battle, were killed. The two women and the driver managed to escape into the wadi. Soon, a British convoy appeared on the scene and attacked the gang, and captured two of them.) The road goes down to Nahal Kelah and crosses it in a concrete bridge. The continuation of Nahal Kelah is Nahal Gallim, which emerges from the hill near Tirat Karmel and pours into the sea near Kefar Gallim. A glance to the west shows the mouth of the river and its beautiful cliffs. The northern cliff is delightful, so take a long look at it and at the fine canyon beside it. Near the bridge to the left of the road is Me'arat Kelah, a cave, used by shepherds to rest their flocks.

Before reaching the top, turn around and look over the cliffs below. The special scenery of the river inspired people to give it names such as "the disappearing valley" (and because in Israel there are several disappearing valleys, this is the "disappearing valley of the Carmel") or, by those who exaggerate, "little Switzerland."

The path brings you out to the beginning of the approach road to Kibbutz Bet Oren from Road 672. Nearby is the Pitulim Campsite and a little to the south of it ancient quarries and other landscapes.

▲
Rock rose, also known as "rose of the Carmel"

▶ Nahal Kelah (Little Switzerland), the Kelah spring

Skeletetons, Skulls, and Women's Lib at
ME'AROT KARMEL (the Carmel Caves)

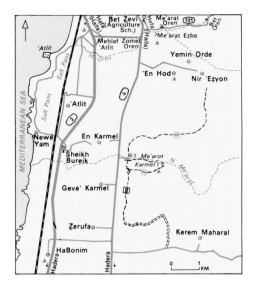

Road 4 is the old road between Hadera and Haifa. To the east of the road you will notice the mouths of many caves. Slow down when you reach kilometers 186-187, and turn, following the signs, to the carpark and the foot of the cliffs at Nahal Me'arot. Bring a flashlight.

Caves and empty spaces, openings into the hillside or the belly of the earth — what could be more fascinating, or mysterious? I cannot offer the entire range of these experiences on this trip, only a cave, or caves.

A few stories, a little imagination, a flashlight or candles — and they are yours. If the mother of the family is connected in some way with the Women's Movement or something similar — then this destination will suit her.

After you get organized at the carpark, climb up to the large cave which has openings shaped like a camel. This is Me'arat Hanahal (the River Cave). The entire river is called Nahal Me'arot (River of the Caves). Go in through the opening and look out from it. If you have a camera with you this is a good frame for a photograph. (If you want to be like everybody else, place the children at the small opening and photograph them facing outwards. Mark the spot where they stand and the place the photographer stands. Then come back here every year and photograph from exactly the same spot, and you will have a measure of your children's growth . . . .) After the viewing and the photographing, go inside. The length of the cave is about 70 meters and with a flashlight you can advance inside and discover that in fact there is no treasure here.

Near this cave there are others — the Tannur (Oven) Cave, Gamal (Camel) Cave, and Gedi (Kid) Cave. These caves have a different story. Today you will find no treasure in them either, but there was a treasure found here in the past . . . . Years ago, when this area was being scouted for stone to build the port of Haifa, the remains of a prehistoric settlement were discovered. Garrod, an archaeologist who was digging elsewhere in the country, was invited to excavate here along with Bight, an anthropologist. Their expedition worked here for several seasons. A movement in England which advocated equal rights for women undertook to help the operation. There was one specific condition: The work on the dig would be done by women only. And that's how it was. Human skeletons and animal remains, tools, ornaments, and other items were found in the cave. Several years ago an archaeological expedition returned here, and this time, men were allowed to join the crew. Many additional finds were uncovered, and there are undoubtedly still more as yet undetected.

Briefly — this was the home of early man. Here he sat around the fire with his family, throwing out leftovers (no problems of taking out the trash). In the neighboring field he gathered his food; the river that flowed nearby apparently served as a fish market . . . .

The excavations, as we said, revealed many finds. If you are curious and want to add to your knowledge, to learn when and how early man lived, and what he was like, it's worth going to Gan Ha'em in Haifa, where there is a large prehistoric display. You can also tour the surroundings. The path marked in blue ▭ will take you up to the ridge; a bit of climbing but a wonderful view of the Carmel Coast.

▲
Me'arat Hanahal (River cave) at Nahal HaMe'arot

▶ A cliff at Nahal HaMe'arot near the Carmel Caves

"A Geyser" and an Eroded Beach at
NEWÉ YAM

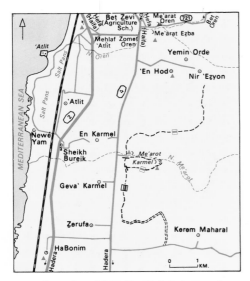

Travel on the old Haifa–Tel-Aviv Road, Road 4, and take Mehlaf Atlit (Intersection) on Road 2 in the direction of Atlit and Newé Yam. Your destination is the section of coast from Newé Yam southwards.

Before getting involved in concepts such as erosion and fissures let's say one thing: The waves are to blame.

One of the phenomena that catch the eye here is the limestone surface on which the waves burst as the tide ebbs and flows. Geographers call this surface an erosion table, and it is found at the edge of limestone ridges such as are found at the seashore. The upper part of the ridge serves as a footpath, while the lower part is under the influence of the waves. The waves act on the table and try to level it, and every few minutes you can see their untiring efforts. This is what has formed the horizontal shape of the table, with its slight incline towards the sea. Near the land is an escarpment that blocks the waves, and another, smaller, escarpment goes down from the table to the sea. Many swimmers who have tried to climb up onto the erosion table have been swept back into the water by the waves. In addition to the visible table, there are others that go down like steps to the sea. When the water is clear they, too, are visible.

The erosion table is not always smooth and flat. The water and the flora and fauna on the erosion table, have produced various forms through dissolution, broad funnels or small boulders creating rugged surfaces. Fissures can be distinguished in the water — in forms such as half-pipes — created by the waves striking the rock. There are also pits and caves. Sometimes an underwater pipe joins the mouth of a deep crater. Picture what happens: The waves push the water through the pipe and it is jetted upwards through the funnel. The water spurts skywards in jets like a geyser.

You can see such a "geyser" at the coast of Newé Yam. Here, to the south of the kibbutz, near the bathing beach, is a concrete dam. This dam is a relic of the plan to build a jetty and perhaps even a port for pre-state illegal immigrants . . . . Beyond the channel is a limestone ridge. If you are lucky, you can see from far off the jets of water spurting upwards from the "belly of the earth." Here the sea water is compressed and bursts upwards through the cracks. The bigger the wave, the higher the "geyser." Therefore, small waves are better than a quiet sea, but if the sea is stormy its waves flood the limestone surface and the "geyser" doesn't work . . . .

The name "geyser" is not correct, of course, in this case. A real geyser bursts from the belly of the earth as a result of pressure, such as one that comes in contact with heat deep inside the earth and emerges in bursts of steam. The most photographed and perhaps the most famous geyser is "Old Faithful" in Yellowstone Park in the United States, but it is not an only child there, and several other young geysers leap alongside it. If you haven't seen "Old Faithful" this one will suffice until you do.

Erosion Table Beach south of Newé Yam

▶ The Newé Yam "Geyser"

Underground Training Camp at
KEFAR SHUMI (Shuni)

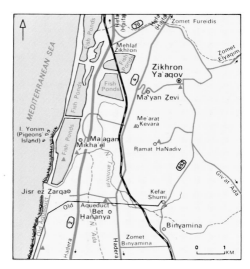

Travel on road 652 from Binyamina to Zikhron Ya'aqov, east of the southern edge of the Carmel. Between kilometers 7-8, to the west of the road, stands a building and several palms. These are the ruins of Shuni.

The name Shuni probably means wheat silo; but this is a relatively new name. About one hundred years ago, when a survey was taken in Palestine by the British Palestine Exploration Fund, the place was marked by the name Mayumas and the sketch of a Roman theater was drawn on the plan. Besides the remains of the theater, other antiquities were found, among them burial caskets, a mosaic floor, and a marble pillar with an inscription on it.

You will not see all these here. In the hundred years since the theater was sketched, some of the stones have been taken away and perhaps you can find some of them in buildings in the vicinity. The Shuni or Shumi building stands on the remains of the theater, and an arch of the remains of the theater and its seats are visible.

With the beginning of modern settlement here, the Shuni lands were purchased together with the surrounding lands and designated for building a new settlement. The new settlement was to symbolize a turning point in the settlement methods of the famous philanthropist Baron Rothschild. In 1914, when Rothschild passed through here, he crossed a bridge over Nahal Tanninim, and said to his companions: "We must establish a mixed settlement here — settlers with private capital and those using my money — so that a settlement like Petah Tiqwa can develop."

The serious obstacle to the realization of the settlement plans was the neighboring Kabara swamp, which has not yet been drained. The local residents, Bedouins from the Gharwarna tribe, opposed drainage although the swamp took a heavy toll in casualties among them. At first the guard of the Shuni lands lived here. Afterwards a group of farmers lived in the Shuni courtyard. The journeys of the Baron led them to call the place after him, Givat Binyamin.

From a document written after World War I, we read of the settlement at Shuni in these words: "It is about six months since the village passed into Jewish hands. Now 25 workers labor here, among them 10 from Zikhron Ya'aqov, who belong mostly to the Gideon Society. Many groups passed through the place and after World War I Shuni became an agricultural training center for settlement candidates."

At the end of the Mandate period the building and its courtyard served as a training ground for the IZL, Irgun Zvai Leumi, a Jewish underground organization that operated during this period. It also served as a base for underground activities in the area. A group of trainees from the organization were caught near here, and the group that broke into Acre jail came from here.

You can go in and visit, identify the location of the theater, and go up to the second floor and the gallery which overlooks the many vineyards in the area — the "raw material" for the wine of Zikhron Ya'aqov.

▲
The inner arch, remnant of the Roman theater

► The "castle" at Shuni village

Fowl at the Fish Ponds at
NAHAL TANNINIM (Crocodile River)

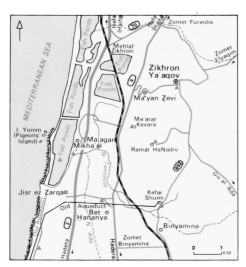

Turn off the old Haifa–Tel Aviv Road, Road 4, between kilometers 173-174 in the direction of Kibbutz Ma'agan Mikhael. Turn to the left before the entrance to the kibbutz, onto a road that leads to the carpark of the Nahal Tanninim Nature Reserve.

Although the subject here is crocodiles, most people come here to the fish ponds in order to see the birds! This tour should be done with a guide and preferably in winter, when there are many birds visiting.

Where are the crocodiles that gave the river its name? And what do crocodiles have to do with Israel anyway?

Many stories are told of the river and the source of its name, and here is one of them: There were once two brothers in Caesaria. Relations between them were very poor and one of them decided to do away the other. He knew his brother went down to bathe in the river every day as a cure for a severe illness. So he brought crocodiles from the Nile in Egypt, put them in the river, and his hated brother was devoured!!! And the crocodiles, who became acclimatized to the river, were fruitful and multiplied . . . .

Don't deride legends: There are also eye-witnesses! It is related that at the end of the last century a three-meter long female crocodile was caught in the river with 48 eggs in her stomach. There is also the testimony of the explorer Tristram: "For a long time," he wrote, "I have heard of debates — are there crocodiles in Palestine or not? I heard from Arabs that goats going down to drink in the river are sometimes snatched by the crocodiles. In the vicinity I also saw traces which left no doubt in my mind that a crocodile had indeed visited here." Finally Tristram also received part of a crocodile of which only a few bones and the skull remained. It was 4 meters long and the length of its skull alone was about 48 centimeters.

In addition to these distant testimonies, a few years ago a member of Kibbutz Ma'agan Mikhael found a crocodile tooth near the river. Furthermore, near the mouth of the river there is an ancient mound on which, according to the prevailing explanation, stood the town of Crocodiliopolis. Could there be better proof than this?

Throughout the years, the abundant river water was exploited; there were also many plans for its use which were not executed. One of these was connected with the period when the Kabara swamps were being drained, and there were dreams of using the water to generate electricity — until it was found that the difficulties were too great and one diesel engine could supply the same amount of energy.

But the water was used in another way — to power flour mills. Several flour mills operated along the course of the river and the largest, the Bridge Mill or "Seven Mills," is here beside Ma'agan Mikhael. Before the water could be utilized, a dam had to be built. This permitted the channeling of water to Caesaria. One of the aqueducts to Caesaria which was designed to increase the water supply to the town began here. The source of the water was Nahal Tanninim and its springs, and since it was a little lower than the "client," it was necessary to build a special system for channeling the water to the fields of the town.

A dam was built over the width of the river, approximately 7 meters high, 175 meters long, and 31 meters wide. The dam exists to this day and serves as a "bridge" for crossing over the river.

Presumably, the dam which was designed to supply the aqueduct to Caesaria served also to turn millstones. There are no great differences between its different parts, but it appears that it was first used to power flour mills as early as the third century C.E.

Today you can stroll on the bridge-dam and see the remains of the chute on which the water flowed and powered the mills. Go down to the reserve — almost a jungle of tamarisks. In season, you will find beautiful water flora blooming in the section beside the bridge.

Nahal Tanninim where it continues to the sea (in the background Jisr ez Zarqa village)

▶ The dam at Nahal Tanninim

Straton Tower, Caesaria Maritima, or
QESARI (Caesaria)

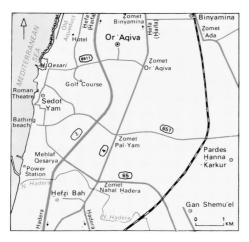

From Road 4, the old Haifa–Tel Aviv Road, turn onto road 6511 towards Or Aqiva and from there to Caesaria. Or, turn off the coastal road, Road 2, at Mehlaf Qesarya, Caesaria Intersection, onto a road leading to the bathing beaches and the site.

We will spare Herod's honor here. About 2,000 years ago he invested a great deal in order to turn a small Hellenistic town called Straton Tower into a large and majestic port city. Its name was Caesari, for Augustus Caesar, and its port was called Sebastus-Augustus. To distinguish it from other towns with similar names, it was called "Caesari Maritima," that is, Caesari by the sea. What did Herod build here? A port city with jetties and warehouses, temples and aqueducts, a hippodrome and a theater, and so on. A short time after Herod's death, Judea was annexed to Syria and the governor resided at Caesari. From then on, it served as the base of the Roman army and the center of its command. The town prospered and at times overshadowed Jerusalem in importance. As major cities there was no room for both Jerusalem and Caesari. The foreigners here became very arrogant and harassed the Jews. Agrippas, Herod's grandson, tried to restore Jerusalem to its glory, but he died. Fights sometimes broke out between Jews and gentiles and according to Josephus, 20,000 Jews were killed here. At the end of the revolt against Rome, Jerusalem was destroyed and Caesari became "primo plavia Augusta Caesaria, capital of princia Judea," in other words, the principal city in Palestine! The Jews of Caesari took part in the Bar Kokheva revolt. The Ten Martyrs were put to death here, among them Rabbi Akiva, one of the leaders of the anti-Roman underground. (The neighboring settlement of Or Aqiva is called after him.)

The place also has a Christian connection. In the days of Governor Felix the Christian missionary Paul, that is, Simon of Tarsus, was arrested here and sent to Rome. In the third century there was a Christian school and library here run by one of the church fathers, and in the fourth century Avesbius, a Christian scholar who wrote the *Onomastikon*, a work of identification of sites in Israel, lived here.

Caesari reached its peak in the Byzantine period, and in the seventh century it was conquered by the Arabs. In the Crusader period it again hit the headlines. It was fortified like all the coastal towns, and like other towns it changed hands several times in battle, until it was finally destroyed by the Mamelukes in 1291. Since then it has stood desolated. The walls that can be seen today are the remains of the fortifications of Louis IX, one of the last organizers of the Crusades. When the wall was destroyed the city was looted. Thousands of stones were taken from it to build other towns and their "representatives" can be found in Jaffa, Altit, Haifa, and Akko. In the nineteenth century a small Moslim village arose here. These were Bosnian emigrants who settled in the ruins and lived here until 1948. To the south of the site Kibbutz Sedot Yam arose and became a training place for Palyam (Israeli Naval underground), a landing area for "illegal" immigrant ships.

To the north of the site is the seashore, the remains of aqueducts, a bathhouse, and so forth. Between the golf course and the Crusader city is the Hippodrome, and to its west, near the carpark, part of the excavated Byzantine road. In this part there is a mosaic, remains of shops, and two statues in secondary use that were placed here on an improvised pedestal by the Byzantines. To the north of the Crusader walls are the remains of a synagogue and two round towers from the fortifications of Straton Tower, which preceded Herod's city.

It is interesting to tour the Crusader port which was built over the old port. Blocks strengthened with Roman columns collapsed after an earthquake and lie near the passage to the port.

To the south of the site is the Roman theater. Watching an evening performance is a great experience, especially if it is a good performance and if it is a moonlit night.

▲
A statue in secondary use in the Byzantine street at Qesari

▶ The remains of the Crusader port at Qesari

Remains of the Citadel and a Jetty at
APOLLONIA

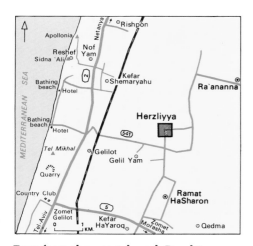

Turn from the coastal road, Road 2, towards Nof Yam and drive west. Just before the end of the road, turn north towards Apollonia, or to the Sidna Ali Mosque, where there is a carpark. Walk north past the youth village and climb up the fenced mound on its eastern slope. Look around then and go down to the shore to see the remains of the Apollonia port. Return to the carpark via the path which leads to a little gorge at the southern edge of the port. About 30 meters from the coast, turn right and climb up a narrow canyon and you will be back in the carpark.

A few years ago it was still possible to clearly discern the remains of the Crusader port of Apollonia. Today the fortress is in ruins and parts of it have collapsed onto the beach, creating an interesting site — pillars, parts of a wall, and sea.

In Crusader times Apollonia was a port; nearby there was a famous battle field. In the tenth century there was a small town here called Arsuf. When the Crusaders arrived about 900 years ago the indigenous population tried to resist them. But the Crusader, Baldwin I, who later became King of Jerusalem, was victor. He was assisted by a Genoese fleet which laid siege to the town from the sea, and defeated it. Apollonia later served Baldwin as a base from which he went out to conquer Jaffa.

Like all Crusader towns, Apollonia changed hands several times. After the defeat of the Crusaders in the battle of the Horns of Hittin (1187), it was conquered by the Moslim Saladdin, but in 1191 a new Crusade landed in Palestine and one of its leaders was the English King, Richard the Lion-hearted, who captured it back from the Moslims.

The "Battle of Arsuf" was a fierce encounter between the soldiers of Richard the Lion-Hearted, whose rear was at Apollonia-Arsuf, and the Moslim soldiers, whose base and support was Mirabel, which is Migdal Afeq. The Crusaders were victorious in this battle too, but before many years had passed Apollonia was again conquered, this time by the Mameluke sultan, Babers. Again the battle was fierce. In those days there was still a forest in the Sharon. Its trees were cut down to serve as supports in the tunnels that were dug beneath the walls of the fortress. "The battle of the tunnels" raged for a long time — the Moslims digging beneath the walls and the Christians trying to destroy and disrupt their work. Finally the fortress fell and the fate of Arsuf was like that of the other coastal towns: Systematic destruction by Babers and his heirs with the intention of preventing the Crusaders from returning to establish themselves here again.

There are meager remains discernible on the mound: a water cistern, a moat — this was the ditch that surrounded the center of the fortress — and another inner fortification. There are also walls and blocks that fell onto the beach. At low tide it is possible to see the remains of the jetties, which are being worn away from day to day. In the southern part of the fortress several sheds have been built, and the building work has certainly not contributed to the beauty of this part of the coast. Among the sheds is the path that leads back to the carpark.

Bathers on the beach near Apollonia

▶ The ruins of Arsuf fortress on the seashore

108

A Fortress and Antiquities at
TEL AFEQ

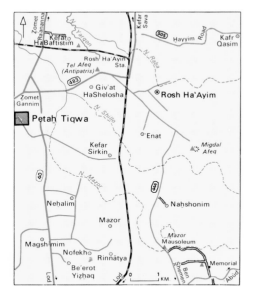

Drive east from Petah Tiqwa on Road 483 in the direction of Rosh Ha'Ayin. Between kilometers 2-3, turn left towards the old railway station, the park, and the site. The remains of structures on the mound can be seen at the turnoff.

Almost fifty years ago, in order to provide work for Jewish laborers, money was collected and used to build the railway line from Ras-El-Ayin, that is, Rosh Ha'Ayin, to Petah Tiqwa. Behind the railway station is the park, and between it and the ancient site, there are abandoned concrete structures, some of which look like watchtowers. Until a few years ago there were signs here indicating that the structures were associated with the municipality of Jerusalem!

What has the municipality of Jerusalem to do with the Rosh Ha'Ayin?

In the thirties, the British Mandatory authorities decided to develop a project that would bring water from the Yarqon River to Jerusalem. The idea was implemented in 1934-5, and the water began to make its way from the springs of Rosh Ha'Ayin to Jerusalem through a pipe 60 kilometers long and 18" in diameter. In order to "push" the water up the hill, several pumping stations were built: at Rosh Ha'Ayin, in the Ayyalon Valley west of Latrun, on the road going up Sha'ar HaGay, and near the Arab village of Saris, which is today Shoeva station. The building at Rosh Ha'Ayin was the first station. During the War of Independence, the enemy took Rosh Ha'Ayin and the Latrun pumping station, and the water ceased flowing to Jerusalem.

Go up to the mound, walk the length of the wall, and go into the courtyard. The fortress is sometimes mistakenly called "The Fortress of Antipatros," and is sometimes even marked on the map by this name. The source of the error lies in the reputation of the town of Antipatros which was built here by King Herod in honor of his father, and which apparently stood on Tel Afeq. But the fortress now visible is from a later period. Afeq is mentioned as far back in history as 4,000 years ago, in the Egyptian "cursed texts." It is listed in the records of Thutmose III (the Egyptian king who conducted many military campaigns in Palestine in the middle of the Second Millenium B.C.E.).

In the Crusader period a fortress stood here called "Castle of the Silent Springs." Later, at the end of the thirteenth century, when the Mamelukes conquered the land, the Sultan Kalaun built a roadside inn here, which became a fortress in the Turkish period. The structure began to fall apart during World War I. The Turks used its stones for building and for the railway line. Fortunately, one of the residents of Petah Tiqwa protested to the Turkish pasha, and the destruction stopped. But not for long. During the British Mandate the structure was again exploited as a supplier of stone. In recent years restoration began on those walls which had remained intact.

In the past excavations were conducted here in connection with works around the water project to Jerusalem. In 1972, serious digging was begun at Tel Afeq, providing more details about its history. To the north of the hillock 3,000-year old remains were unearthed, including structures and a brick wall and a palace. In one of the corners fragments of clay tablets were discovered, written in hieroglyphics and including a list of terms, a kind of "phrase book," perhaps for the king's clerks at Afeq. There is evidence of a great fire and destruction 2,300 years ago, and in later strata there are signs of Philistines, and then Israelites. These remains are near the western gate of the structure in the courtyard and on the slope. To the south of the Turkish structure a stone-paved Byzantine street was exposed, and beside it the remains of shops. The paved section is impressive.

From the top of the hill there is a view of the Rosh Ha'Ayin springs (these have mostly been trapped and brought ignominiously in pipes), and in the morning there is a good view to the west.

End of May blooms at the Yarqon near Afeq

▶ A corner tower at Afeq Fortress

Preferably in the Morning, at
MIGDAL AFEQ

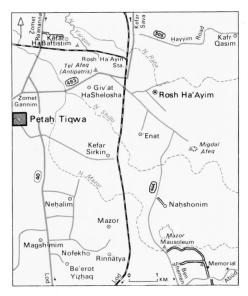

Drive east from Petah Tiqwa on Road 483 in the direction of Rosh Ha'Ayin, and then on Road 444, which is its continuation. Between kilometers 19-20 a road leads up to an improvised parking area near the entrance to Afeq Castle. It's very hard to go wrong: The castle rises above you!

Migdal Tzedek, Migdal Afeq, Migdal Yabah, Mirabel are all names of the group of structures that stand on a hill 140 meters above sea level. The place hasn't yet been thoroughly excavated, and its history can only be discerned from the structures and stones which are visible on the surface. From the top of the hill in front of the entrance to the building, the fortress on Tel Afeq can be clearly seen and the width of the passage connecting the two precisely assessed.

The Arabic name of the tower is Majdal Tzadek, after the eighteenth-century Sheikh Tzadek El-Jamaini, who revolted against the Turkish reign which then prevailed in Palestine. Years later the Turks banished him, but his name remained. Another name often used by the Arabs is Majdal Yabah, and there are some who see a connection between Yabah and Jaffa, in other words, a Majdal near Jaffa.

The Crusaders called the place Mirabel, meaning "beautiful surprise" — because of the beautiful view. And this is one of the best places to view the Sharon. The morning hours, when the sun lights up the scene from the east, offer the best view.

Various building styles will be distinguishable even to the untrained eye. In the north-west corner of the structure, large ancient stones, light in color, are set into the newer parts of the structure. The central structure of Migdal Tzedek is from an earlier period, apparently Roman. On the right is a wall built of large stones. Additions from later periods are discernible at its sides; relatively "new" walls border on the central square.

On the large wall there is a low opening with signs of the door bolt. Above the opening is a large stone which was brought here, and on it is an inscription telling of the "place of death of St. Kyrikus." Go inside. Here there is a hall and a staircase going up to another floor.

Now go back to the central courtyard. From here steps lead up to the second storey. Make your way carefully to the western wing. Through the windows to the west the Sharon landscape appears in all its beauty.

From here you can see Tel Afeq, and can understand the meaning of the name "bottleneck" given to the passage between Migdal Tzedek and Tel Afeq. From the Yarqon springs and westwards from there to the sea, the river formed a difficult topographical obstacle. There were periods when passage was made even more difficult by surrounding swamps. To the east of the springs the Samarian hills begin to rise, and between the springs and the hills a narrow passage is formed, called "Afeq Pass."

Fortresses were erected here to control the road, and sometimes other fortification lines were established to obstruct passage. Josephus writes in his book, *The Jewish Wars:* "And again trouble was made by Antiochus . . . when the latter went out to fight with the Arabs. Alexandros feared him and dug a deep trench the entire length of the country, between the hills near Antipatros and the coast of Jaffa. And beside the ditch he built a high wall with wooden towers on it to close the gates of the land." Alexander Yanai tried, therefore, to block the Afeq Pass. He didn't succeed, and Antiochus managed to fill in the "crack" and continue on.

During World War I, the British were held up near the Yarqon in their military campaign in Palestine. In September 1918 Allenby broke through the fortification line. His forces circumvented Afeq Pass from the east, attacked the Turks at Jaljulia, defeated them, and continued on in a rapid advance northwards. On both sides of the pass, as we mentioned, there are fortresses, and one of them is the fortress of Tel Afeq.

▲
Afeq Castle — a view from the west

▶ The inner courtyard at Migdal Afeq

The Revolt Broke Out at
MODI'IM

If you are in the town of Lod, simply turn towards Ben Shemen, cross Road 1 using the flyover, and continue towards Road 443. You can also travel from Ben-Gurion airport eastward on Road 453 until it bisects Road 444 and south to the junction with Road 443. Sound complicated? If you look at the map on page 95 you'll see it's quite simple.

Do you know who Antiochus Epiphanes was?

There are some who spit when they hear the name of this evil man and I don't think he has many fans among Jews. As he is not popular with us we will mention him only briefly, just enough for our purposes: This tyrant was the king of Syria and a descendant of Alexander the Great, whose officials came to Modi'im where they built an altar to the Greek god Zeus. Their attempt to force the people of Modi'im and Mattathias the Hasmonean to sacrifice on their altar was met with refusal by Mattathias, who in response declared a revolt. This was the continuation of a process that had begun earlier and found expression in the deteriorating relations between the Jews and the alien rulers of Palestine, culminating in 167 B.C.E. in the revolt known to us as the Maccabean revolt. The place where the revolt broke out is thought to be Modi'in, which is identified today as near the village of Midia.

Did we say Modi'in? What about Mudait or Modi'im?

Well, this renewed acquaintance of ours with Antiochus raises several questions, and since I have begun I will both ask and answer.

First question — why so many names? We must decide: Modi'im, Modi'in, or Mudait! We have decided: Modi'im! But in the sources, the other names also appear. A Christian bishop named Avesbius who lived here in the fourth century worked on the identification of ancient places and he wrote in his book, *Onomastikon,* that Modi'im is a "village near Lod." An ancient map which was discovered in the town of Medva east of the Jordan (on a mosaic floor) shows a house with two towers at its sides, and beside it is written in Greek, "Modi'im today Modaita, from where the Maccabees came." Although excavations have not been conducted here, many think that the same Modi'im was on a hill bearing the name E-Ras (the head). This hill, as we said, is near the village of Midia, which perhaps suggests the name Modi'im. Some scientists have tried to identify the location of Modi'im and the family grave of the Hasmonean house, which was supposed to be here. In the Book of Maccabees it says: "And Simon built a headstone on the grave of his father and brothers, high to look at, of hewn stone front and back, and he put seven pyramids next to each other, to his father, his mother, and the four brothers, with artwork on them and he placed large columns around. This is the grave he made at Modi'im to this day." Explorers sought the grave and did not find it, and we have apparently lost the possibility of a "tour of the pyramids" not far from Tel Aviv. But there are some who claim to have seen the remains of structures and perhaps the base of the splendid gravestone near the grave of Sheikh El-Gharbawi beside the "Kubur El-Yahud" (the graves of the Jews).

From here we come to the second question and its answer: Where is "Kubur El-Yahud"? This is it! These are the graves which for years have been shown as the graves of the Maccabees. On the hillock cut into the rock are several graves and among them stand out nine which are cut in a row and above them large stones covering them, but who will "guarantee" that these are really the graves of the Maccabees? No one.

Near the place, at the top of the hillock, stands a monument in memory of the IDF soldiers who fell in the region.

▲
The "graves of the Maccabees" at Modi'im

▶ The fire prevention post at Modi'im

The Whys of the Name
SHOMERON (Sebaste)

Take Road 57, the Nablus–Tulkarm Road. About 10 kilometers west of Shekhem (Nablus), turn off on Road 60 towards Jenin. That's it. Some 2 kilometers from Zomet Deir Sharef (Junction), between kilometers 160-161, a narrow road turns right (there is a signpost) and up to Sebaste.

You are headed for a royal city, once one of Israel's capitals. The historical story is flattering to Jews, the finds on the spot even more so. The visual remains here are mostly the work of gentiles, and they are beautiful.

The main story of the site begins when Omri, King of Israel, sought a place for his capital. He found a strategic site, bought the plot, and named it after its former landlord. Evidence of this? Book of Kings I, Chapter 16, Verse 24: ". . . And he called the name of the city which he built, after the name of Shemer, owner of the hill, Samaria [Shomeron]." The town stretched over a large area (some 25 acres) and had a fortress and a royal palace. Until its destruction it served as the capital of Israel. The name of the capital was given to the entire region and thus we have Samaria.

And what about Sebaste? After the city was destroyed it was rebuilt. We will skip the history of the Hellenistic period, mention only that King Yanai began settling it, but it was mostly built and reglorified by Herod, when it was given to him as a gift by the Roman Emperor Augustus. (What a gift!) Herod built the city as only he knew how to build and called it by the name given to his benefactor. Sebastus means "the magnificent" and this was Augustus' nickname. The city passed through additional metamorphoses, was destroyed and rebuilt, and even the Crusaders reached here and left some of their buildings.

And what can you see of all this?

Right at the entrance there are two impressive round watchtowers whose bases are Hellenistic. From here there is the imposing road of pillars some 12 meters wide and one kilometer long. Six hundred pillars were unearthed here during the archaeological excavations. Some of them still stand in their original places; nearby are the remains of the shopping arcade.

The carpark is near another group of pillars — this is the Roman forum, the urban center of those days. Among the many pillars are some that stand on one tip of the base. This was apparently the assembly place of the city dignitaries, and perhaps also the lawcourt.

The path leads to the remains of the theater where the spectators' seats, the aisles, and part of the orchestra floor have been exposed. The theater was built in the third century C.E. Above it are the remains of a round watchtower which has been well-preserved and is older than the theater by many years! At the top of the mound are remains of a temple to the Emperor Augustus built by Herod. Broad steps lead up to it; the entrance was through impressive rows of pillars.

The remains of Israelite Samaria are less impressive. The ruins of the king's palace and the fortifications were excavated and are to the south of the temple. Here a treasure of ivories and potsherds were found, with inscriptions on them telling of the period.

Continuing round the mound you will pass a small church, get a good view of the region, and then return to the forum.

Among the houses of the Arab village of Sebastiya there are additional remains: large sarcophagi and the ruins of a Byzantine church and a Crusader cathedral (here, it is believed, lies the head of John the Baptist). If you climb up to the mosque at the corner of the structure you can enjoy a good view of the village and the surroundings.

▲
"The grave of St. John" at the village of Sebastiya

▶ The road of pillars in Shomeron (Sebaste)

Orchards and Swimming Pools at
NAHAL QANA

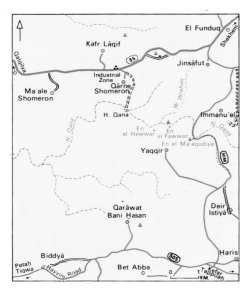

The Qarne Shomeron settlement is reached via Road 55 from Qalqilya to Shekhem (Nablus). After looking around the settlement go down Wadi Halat El-Bala to Nahal Qana and walk upstream. Tour the river, springs, and pools and either go back the way you came, or go on to En Ma'aqudiya — but only if you have a car waiting for you on the road.

Hollyhocks

Until a few years ago, no one ever noticed Nahal Qana. At most, people crossed over it on a bridge on the Petah Tiqwa–Ramatayim Road. What was there to see anyway, just a dry river course and the suggestion of a bridge . . . .

But Wadi Qana, or Nahal Qana by its Hebrew name, is one of the "notables" of Samaria, both because of its length and because of its beauty and its springs. Its source is near the Jerusalem–Nablus road in the Mikhmetat Valley. From here, like all rivers, it flows to the sea, but it doesn't use the shortest route. It pours into the Yarqon River and "takes a lift" with it to the sea. In biblical times Nahal Qana served as a border marker between the region of the tribe of Ephraim and the tribe of Menashe and a road even went through here. Nahal Qana also has springs, the remnants of a forest, and something like bathing pools in the river course, and on its banks irrigated agriculture. Any one of these would be a good reason to come here; but the main thing is just to get here.

The easy way to get down to Nahal Qana is from the approach road to Qarne Shomeron. A few score meters before the entrance a dirt road turns left and continues parallel with Wadi Halat El Bala — named because of holes (*bala* in Arabic) in the river bank — taking us to Nahal Qana. Here the feast of water begins, with orchards, greenery, and landscapes.

Walk up the river to the east. After about 300 meters, at "the corner" of Wadi Sha't and Nahal Qana are the ruins of Qana. Not much is left of the ruins, which stretch over a small area: There are remains of structures, walls, and nearby, several new houses. Apparently the biblical name Qanah was preserved here, leading to the Arabic name of the river — Wadi Qa'ana. The dirt road continues eastwards and later becomes a path. First there is a pumping station with a small pool at its feet. After this the river flows and the puddles of water become pools when the opportunity arises.

The scenery along the river changes with the seasons of the year. For example, at the end of April there is a collection of Mesopotamian irises between the road and a citrus grove very near to the Qana ruins. A little further on, in a pool near En el Hawwar, a surprise may await you: The pool may be occupied by . . . sheep! Once, in passing by here, we saw three shepherds standing in the pool, and on the slope another sturdy shepherd. From time to time the sturdy one pulled a sheep out of the flock and pushed it into the water where the others waited to scrub and wash it . . . . After a "thorough cleaning" accompanied by bleating, crying, and the singing of the shepherds, a clean sheep left the waters and another one was pushed in its place . . . .

But there is hope. The other pools of the river are vacant. The large pool is near En Fawwar and to the meeting of Wadi Ibrahim with Nahal Qana.

The amount of water in the pools changes, of course, according to the season of the year and the amount of rain, but the river, in this part, flows all year round! In summer it irrigates the plots. The water flows in channels and the activity and commotion make a visit well worthwhile. There are also real woods on the slopes. Near En el Ma'aqudiya, next to the road to Yaqqir, there is a wooded slope which was declared a forest reserve back in the days of the British. Do you want to take a trip to Nahal Qana? The answer should be a definite yes.

▶ Touring Nahal Qana

Who's Ever Heard of
DEIR QAL'A

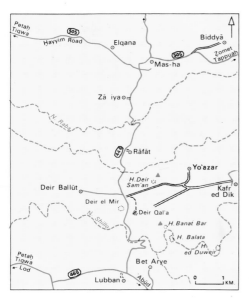

Road 505 from Kafr Qasim is the "Cross-Samaria" road. It can be reached from either Petah Tiqwa or Kefar Sava. Drive until the turnoff onto Road 446 southwards. Pass by several villages and stop a few hundred meters beyond the turnoff to Deir Ballut. A path inside the olive orchard will take you a bit eastward. Now climb up to the remains that you saw from below. It is a steep ascent, and it is a little difficult to find the path, but it's well worth the effort — after 20 minutes you will be at the top, with a fantastic view. These are directions for hikers. But you can come directly by car: Turn east opposite the entrance to Deir Ballut, and after a short distance turn right to a new Jewish settlement that sits directly above Deir Qal'a. From here, it's a short walk.

As the path climbs towards Deir Qal'a, you will pass and undoubtedly admire the little cultivated plots, sometimes 1x1 meter, on the slopes. When you are almost at the top you will see the remains of structures — rooms and walls. On a rock below the main structure there is a cave containing the remains of a church and inside it a small spring with clear water. If you can't find the spring — that means it's the dry season. These things happen. If you can't find the cave, never mind; that happens, too. The main thing is that you reach the top. Among the outstanding remains on the hill are the ruins of a church (this is apparently the source of the name Deir, which means monastery and sometimes church, and Qal'a — citadel). Near the church are plastered pools whose length reaches 30 meters. Another pool is to be found southwest of the church, where there are remains of other structures, too. Meanwhile stay near the church. Some of its stones have disappeared but we know of them from the words of explorers of Palestine in the last century and the sketches they left us. These people were enthusiastic about the structures and wrote that this was "perhaps the most beautiful and well-preserved of the ruined monasteries in Palestine." According to the remains, the age of the structure is dated to the Byzantine period, making it about 1,500 years old. Move around carefully between the walls. You will discern at the south side a hewn channel. This is a moat which was perhaps designed to defend the place. Near it are walls of hewn stone and a window with an interesting frame which serves today as a "substitute door." You can go in through it to one of the rooms.

The entire site is considered a fortified farm whose lands were in the surroundings. View the landscape from the building or go a little south to the edge of the cliff. The view to the west is very beautiful.

If you come here in winter, after a heavy rainfall, you will see an interesting view of the village of Deir Ballut. The village stands in a little valley with no drainage; after the rains it becomes flooded and the village looks like a beautiful island.

▲
The fortified structure at Deir Qal'a

▶ A view from Deir Qal'a to the flooded area near Deir Ballut, photographed during a rainy winter

THE JUDEAN DESERT AND THE JUDEAN HILLS

The Judean Desert is a "local desert." Apart from the fact that it is Israeli, this concept indicates that the conditions of its formation are local and it is not necessarily part of the belt of world deserts. It is "in the shade of the rains," when the Judean mountain block screens the desert in the west and "stops" the clouds. When the clouds do reach it, they plunge down to the lowest place in the world, the Dead Sea, and lose their strength. On a world scale this is a mini-desert. Its width can be crossed on foot in one day. Its nearness to the population centers in the Judean Hills made it a place of seclusion for monks who lived in the desert but were still not too far from their centers in the towns. In particular the desert served as a place of refuge for zealot fighters and rebels. The difference in altitude between the Judean Hills and the Dead Sea Basin is over 1000 meters. On this steep slope the rivers cut deep canyons in the desert and in some of them caves opened up, which served generations of fighters and rebels. Here the story of Massada was played out, here are caves Bar Kokheva's warriors used, here are the remains of a settlement in the En Gedi oasis, and here are guardposts on road sections in the desert. Modern development is biting deeply into the desert, diminishing some of its desert charm. Let the developers leave us a quiet piece of desert to rest in, to attract tourists and hikers to the hotels and to enjoy the services that have been built on the desert path that is left. . .

On the east, the Judean Desert is bordered by the Dead Sea, which is part of it, with its shores and quarries. The south of the Dead Sea is now all evaporation ponds and industrial plants.

There are some who consider the Euphrates River as its border — Nahal Perat, Wadi Qilt in the north, and in the south around the "plug of salt" which is Mt. Sedom. In the west — the Judean Hills, between Jerusalem and Hebron and a little to the south.

In our book we barely have a chance to glance at the Judean Hills and particularly at the section of "corridor" to the west of Jerusalem. This is the strip of hills between the mountain and the coastal plain.

As in Samaria, here, too, crossing the breadth of the country is a variegated trip — from the coastal strip through the plain to the Judean Hills, Jerusalem, and east of it in the Judean Desert to the Dead Sea. What other country can offer such a wide variety over such a small distance?

Very Old and Still Attractive
MIQWE YISRA'EL

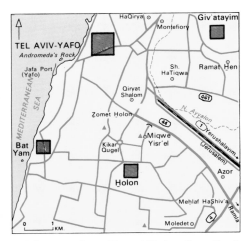

Driving east from Zomet Holon (Junction) on Road 44, the entrance is between kilometers 40-39. The entrance from Holon is through Levi Eshkol Avenue: go around Kikar Halochamim and turn eastward at Qugel Avenue as far as the traffic lights, to the southern gate entrance of Miqwe Yisra'el. (It is closed on Saturdays and holidays.)

People often ask what is so attractive about a 110-year-old? But there's no denying it — at this advanced age Miqwe Yisra'el still looks gorgeous.

Once, before the Jaffa–Jerusalem Road was a busy traffic artery, you could go in through the north gate. An avenue of Washingtonia palms accompanied the arrivals as far as the office buildings and the school. Here Herzl met Kaiser Wilhelm II in 1898, and many years later, when his vision was almost realized, convoys of supplies and passengers made their way through this gate southwards to Jerusalem. They went in through the north gate and out through the south gate, and drove through the sands towards Rishon Le-Zion and to their destination. In the corner near the gate is a pillbox, a memento of those days. But, as required, the entrance today is through the southern gate. A little past the gate a dirt road leads to the grave of Karl Netter, the founder of the agricultural school. Near the grave is the school with its cowshed, sheep pens, hen house, and greenhouses.

Near the carpark which is close to the office buildings, a cave is cut into the limestone ridge. This was the first living quarters of Karl Netter. From here Miqwe Yisra'el began to grow.

Miqwe Yisra'el has come a long way. After Karl Netter's death he was replaced by other principals, and each contributed something to the institution. Studying in a residential agricultural school was a special experience in those days. "Uncle Joshua" Margolin who established the Pedagogical Biological Institute was a famous graduate. Israel's fearful weapon in the War of Independence, the "Davidka," which was merely a large pipe that became a mortar, was built here. And lots and lots of farmers learned all they knew from the school.

The "old center" includes several structures: The winepress which no longer works and which served as a cache for the Hagganah (Jewish resistance), the central building, which contains the synagogue, the school, and library and two staircases leading to a small square and is the meeting place for pupils of the institution. The path bordering on the building is built in a straight line. Karl Netter's house is set among houses built in the style of those days with Parisian designs. The long building had a dining room, sewing room, and cubicles for workers who lived here. The pupils lived on the second floor and near them was the master's apartment. All in one building.

At the end of the building is a water cistern which is the pride of the Miqwaites, and according to them this is the first plastered cistern in Israel. Near the cistern is the tree that has become almost the symbol of Miqwe Yisra'el —the Bengali sycamore, which is a forest composed of a single tree. It, too, is about a hundred years old with hanging roots, and provides shelter to a considerable area.

The highlight of the visit is the botanical garden at the eastern side. In the corners of the garden are monuments to the memory of the seven guards who died on duty in a pick-up truck near here in 1948, and to graduates of the school who fell in Israel's wars. The garden itself is an entire world. Since it was planted in 1930, one hundred and fifteen plant families have been collected here, with one thousand two hundred genera and species. The foliage found here includes medicinal plants, plants used in industry, climbing plants, hedge plants, and eucalyptus. There is a cork oak shaped like a bottle and a tree called a "snake tree." And all of this a few minutes distance from the town and its bustle. Unbelievable.

▲
The Bengali sycamore at Miqwe Yisra'el

▶ The botanical garden at Miqwe Yisra'el

"Valley of Springs" at
CANADA PARK

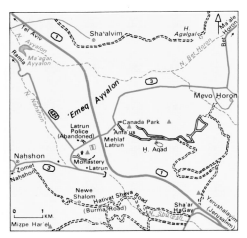

Drive on Road 1, the Tel-Aviv–Jerusalem highway, to Mehlaf Latrun (interchange) and then to Road 3 leading north. Between kilometers 272-273, less than a kilometer from the interchange, is the main entrance to Canada Park, at the edge of the Ayyalon Valley.

The title, "Canada Park," perhaps obliges us to talk about the entire park, but we will make our excuses right from the start — we can't! The park, well-tended by the Jewish National Fund with monies contributed by Canadian Jewry (hence the name), stretches over the entire eastern edge of the Ayyalon Valley and the Judean Hill range which slides down into the valley.

The Ayyalon Valley itself has had its fill of wars in the course of history. It is in a key position on the route to Jerusalem and Joshua Bin-Nun, Judah the Maccabi, the Moslims, the Crusaders all fought here. And in the War of Independence it was the site of bloody battles that culminated in the Ayyalon Valley becoming a no-man's land. During the Six Day War the area fell into Israeli hands. In consequence of the war the villages in this region were abandoned and the land was developed as a park.

The park extends over thousands of acres and includes antiquities and old agricultural projects. On the eastern side, which was opened to the public a few years ago, are the remains of the Crusader fortress, Castellum Arnold, which was built on the old mound of Ayyalon. Dirt roads lead to archaeological remains near Deir Ayub and towards Sha'ar Hagay. Camping sites have been set up on the peaks and in hidden corners.

At Hurvat Aqad, on the ridge which borders the park to the south, remains of a settlement have been unearthed, with fortifications and a hideaway cave characteristic of the Bar Kokheva period.

In a walled-in yard between the interchange and the entrance to the park are the ruins of a Byzantine church and a Crusader church as well as the remains of a Roman house with a mosaic floor. All these are part of Ama'us, which is Hamat, an ancient town whose remains can be seen nearby. Near the site, in a Moslim cemetery, stands a domed building said to be the grave of Sheikh Obeid, but which is in fact a Roman bath-house which has been partly exposed. And this is only a part of what there is to see in the large area of the park.

Its "veteran" core stretches on both sides of Road 3 leading to Ramallah. To the west of the road is the "Hazeitim" campsite, with picnic areas and sports facilities. To the east of the road are observation posts, ancient oil-presses, and paths. The central site in this part is Emeq Hama'ayanot — the Valley of Springs. Here, apparently, are the remains of channels which led to Ama'us 1,700 years ago, when it flourished. The upper channel begins at the head of the valley and the water flows from a tunnel penetrating into the rock. A trench three meters long had to be dug in the lower channel in order to reach the spring that supplied it. In the fall and winter, it is lovely to walk through the vegetation, accompanied by the sound of flowing water. On the way you can see an ancient burial cave and here and there a path leading to a particularly beautiful spot. If the water in the channels has dried up you can console yourself at Ma'ayan Hatmarim (palm spring), which is at the end of the route. This spring gives water all year round and there is a broad grassy area beside it.

▲
En Tmarim (palm spring) — at the west of the park

▶ Emeq Hama'ayanot (valley of springs) at Canada Park

Are They Really Silent at LATRUN?

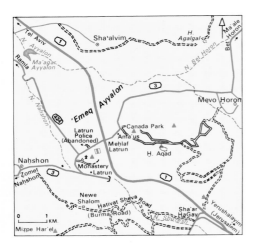

Once the monastery was on the main road to Jerusalem, but when the super highway was opened the monastery was left somewhat to one side. To get there leave the Jerusalem–Tel Aviv Highway, Road 1, at Mehlaf Latrun (interchange), and take Road 3. From here the entrance to the woods and the monastery is between kilometers 270-271.

Tourists call it the monastery of the silent. But if you chance by in the early morning or toward noon, during prayers, you will actually hear the monks speaking after all.... The leaflet handed out by the monks says, "Silence — we are called 'the silent' but our correct name is Trappists. Indeed, we have chosen this life of silence of our own free will.... It brings the monk nearer to God. In certain cases a monk may speak but conversation on religious matters is forbidden, and even more so on secular matters." So what is there left to say?

You will meet a monk at the entrance and in the wine-selling area, but these monks are on duty, and speaking is part of their job. The Trappists meet for prayer seven times a day, from 2:15 a.m. to 7 p.m. After the last prayer they go to bed "in a dormitory for rest, and sleep on their simple beds made of three planks of wood and a straw mattress," as they put it.

The Trappist Order was established in France 800 years ago and today there are dozens of such monasteries and convents throughout the world. Latrun Monastery was established in 1890, damaged in World War I and restored and rebuilt in 1927. Its walls envelop the Maccabi Hotel — a building erected even before the monastery, and which served as a hostel for pilgrims on their way to Jerusalem. In the monastery yard are various buildings, including a wine-cellar whose products are on sale.

You can visit the monastery itself, as well. Go in through a gate to a small, well-tended courtyard and climb up to the second floor. Here you will be above the church and near a balcony that overlooks the Ayyalon Valley.

Relations between the monks of Latrun and the State of Israel existed to some extent before the Six Day War, when part of the monastery land was in Jordan and part in Israel. The part in Israel was worked by Israeli neighbors in exchange for part of the crops. When the entire monastery came into Israeli hands after the Six Day War, contacts between the neighboring kibbutz, Nahshon, and the monastery became closer. One of the kibbutz members learned the craft of stained-glass making from an old monk and does this today at the kibbutz. It is quite possible, therefore, that some day you will come across stained-glass windows in a synagogue made by a kibbutznik who learned his craft from a Christian monk....

The area of the monastery is rich in stories and there are many interesting sites to visit. There is the Ayyalon Valley. And above the monastery there are the remains of a Crusader fortress where Jordanian forces were entrenched and which Israel did not succeed in conquering until the Six Day War. There is also an abandoned police station which was part of the military deployment. Beside the police station and the Crusader fortress are monuments to the fallen of Israel's Seventh Brigade which fought here in 1948.

▲
Remains of the Crusader fortress and Jordanian army trenches at the Latrun fort above the monastery

▶ A view of the monastery from the west

Exile, Holocaust, and Revival in the
SCROLL OF FIRE

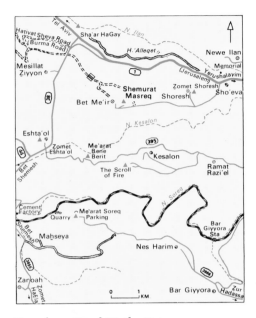

Turn from Road 38, the Bet Shemesh–Sha'ar Hagay Road, to Road 395, the Ramat Raziel Road. Between kilometers 6-7 turn off for Moshav Kesalon. Before reaching the moshav, however, follow the signs and take the narrow road to the Scroll of Fire.

You will be able to discern the scrolls from a distance. A large scroll stands open, ready to be read. The opening into the scroll — through an empty space at the bottom of one of the rolls, serves a dual purpose: It is an entrance and a passage for the wind between the rolls, in order not to upset its balance. The monument is cast in bronze and the sculptor, Nathan Rapaport, worked on it for three and a half years in Italy. When the work was finished it was brought to Israel in two parts, each weighing about seven tons. Other works by Rapaport can be found in Israel — the statue of Mordecai Anilevitz, commander of the Warsaw Ghetto uprising, which stands on the hill of the ruined water tower at Kibbutz Yad Mordekhay, and the statue symbolizing the union of defenders — soldiers and citizens — in the military cemetery at Negba.

But the Scroll of Fire differs from the others in its power and in its form of expression. The reliefs on the parchment-like sections recall walls and pillars from early historical periods when stories were etched or painted. Two stories are depicted on the Scrolls, one the history of the diaspora and the holocaust, and the other the establishment of Israel, with a glance at the distant past.

When you stand facing the monument the story begins on the right-hand roll. At the bottom are the ghetto houses and people on their way to a concentration camp. Among them is the figure of the educator, Dr. Janusz Korchak, going with his pupils to a death camp. Above them, leading in a different direction (upwards) is a depiction of the ghetto fighters, battling the Nazi enemy. German soldiers are portrayed in symbolic form — a steel helmet, a tank — there is no human figure of a Nazi. Above — fighters and simple weapons: Molotov cocktails, a knife, and a large stone thrown at an armored car. Further on — flames and a lamp, camps and a flag. From here there is the departure for Israel in the illegal immigrant ships, and the attempt to gain a foothold in Palestine. On the same roll, in an optimistic scene, various figures radiate confidence. They are going to Palestine and not to the death camps. End of story one.

The second roll depicts Israel and its establishment from the War of Independence to the liberation of Jerusalem in the Six Day War. Again scenes of battle, but in a different atmosphere. A soldier takes leave of a woman and goes off to battle, a new immigrant receives arms and leaves behind his knapsack. There are war scenes, and a scene of a paratrooper weeping at the Western Wall. The second roll ends in a story moving in an upward direction: a lamp held up in a victory procession.

▲
Cyclamen on the Judean Hills

▶ The Scroll of Fire — a view from the west

The First Railway at
NAHAL REFA'IM (Refa'im River)

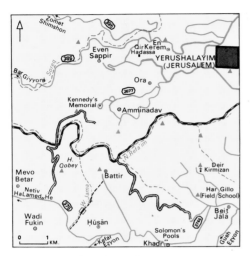

Leave Jerusalem from the west, pass Bet Hakerem and Qiryat haYovel, and take Road 3877, in the direction of Moshavim Ora and Amminadav. Before Moshav Ora, a road turns off, bypassing the moshavim and leading to the Kennedy Memorial and Mount Amminadav. Dirt tracks branching off from this road lead to spectacular views of Nahal Refa'im, Kefar Battir, and the surroundings. Searching for a lookout point is an outing all in itself.

Nahal Refa'im is a tributary of Nahal Soreq and is exceptional among the rivers that make their way from the Judean Hills to the Mediterranean Sea. Like the others, its origins are in the hills north of Jerusalem, but from here its streams wind in different directions. One central stream is Nahal Bet Hanina, which begins near the village of Bet Hanina north of Jerusalem. A section of this stream is "famous": It crosses the Jerusalem Highway at the "dangerous curve" at Moza, and then accompanies the road in its deep bed, between Jerusalem and Ramot and Nabi Samwil. This is the main stream and is honored with the name Nahal Soreq. It is joined by Nahal Samuel, Nahal Atarot, and others.

Another large stream is Nahal Refa'im, which begins in Jerusalem at Emeq Refa'im. (*Refaim* are mentioned in the Book of Genesis as the early inhabitants of Israel — spirits of the dead or extinct giants.) It was here that David fought the Philistines and defeated them in his early days as king of Jerusalem. The railway line going up to the capital from the coast runs in the course of this stream. The stream descends in curves and meets Nahal Soreq at the interscction of Har Hatayyasim in the north, Har Pitulim in the west, Har Soreq, and Har Giyyora. At this junction there is a bridge over which the road to Nes Harim and Bar Giyyora passes. From here Nahal Soreq winds in broad curves which have given various landscape explorers a great deal of work. They tried to discover the meaning of this behavior, and the problem has never been fully solved. The visible result — many curves and therefore a long but very gradual ascent from the coast and the plain to the mountain. The railway exploits this advantage. At the end of the last century the first railway line in the country was laid in the riverbed to Jerusalem. Years later the lines were changed and the system was improved but the train still travels slowly up the hill, looking from above like a toy train.

Many stories are connected with Nahal Refa'im. Until the Six Day War the armistice line between Israel and Jordan was parallel to the railway line. The rail line actually delineated the border. The village of Battir stood on the Jordanian side while its lands were in Israel. The Battir railway station had special status. It was in Israeli territory, but the train did not stop there . . . .

Today you can tour the entire area. There are dirt roads going down from Ora and Amminadav to Nahal Soreq, and another dirt road parallel with Nahal Refa'im. With some good advice and a suitable map you can roam around here quite a lot.

▲
The railway station at Battir

▶ A view of Nahal Refa'im

The Works of Nature at
SOREQ CAVE

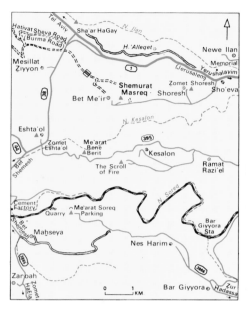

The Soreq Cave in the Absalom Reserve can be reached from the Bar Giyyora–Nes Harim area. Take Road 386 from En Kerem, or Road 375 which connects the Ela Valley with Mount Hebron. On Road 386 turn west near Bar Giyyora to Road 3866 and then follow the signs on the road that bypasses the settlements and goes to the Absalom Reserve. The reserve can also be reached by road from Bet Shemesh and Mahseya. Today, this is the main entrance.

▲
A Sight at Soreq Cave

Until an explosion in 1968 in the Har-Tuv quarry, the stalactite caves in the region of Ma'arat Hateomim (twin caves) was *the* cave. When the new cave was discovered at the edge of the quarry people began creeping, in more senses than one, to the place. They were eager to see the treasure that had been unearthed. There was neither a path nor lighting and in the dark the large chamber looked huge and frightening and seemingly endless. To prevent stalactites and stalagmites from being damaged the entrance was closed with iron doors and when these didn't succeed in preventing uninvited guests, a large pile of rocks was heaped at the entrance. Work then began on planning organized visits.

When the cave was opened to the public everyone agreed that the waiting had been worthwhile. Suitable lighting and a "floating" path made it a hit. It took months to get tickets.

Now the visit is made in comfort. As you sit at the entrance adjusting your eyes to the darkness of the cave, you will see an audio-visual film telling of the formation of the cave and its treasures. Then you will go into the "palace" itself. The cave's dimensions seem large, but are minute in comparison with world-famous stalactite caves. Nevertheless, the experts say that this one is one of the most beautiful in the world. It's true there are no kilometer-long paths deep in the earth, nor is there a subterranean lake, but there are stalactites of all kinds.

The cave is over 90 meters long and about 80 meters wide. Altogether it is some 5,000 square meters. To this day, during the rains and after them, the ceiling drips. The remains of a snake were found here; apparently it had come through burrows penetrating through the roof.

The formation of stalactites, stalagmites and their accessories does not happen overnight. For millions of years the water does its work. The "public relations" work and the publicity for their actions are done by other natural forces: As a result of internal activity or a river cutting through a hillside or erosion by water, caves or empty spaces form in the rock. Water drips in the cave and sometimes the water, accompanied by carbon dioxide (added to it from the air on the way to its task) continues to seep through the rock and drip in the still-blocked cavities in the caves.

And this is the process of formation of stalactites and stalagmites. A drop of water, and with it dissolved limestone, drips from the ceiling of the cave. The drop evaporates before it reaches the floor and the dissolved limestone remains as a spot on the ceiling. Another drop, and more dissolved limestone, and so, slowly, from inside the ceiling a column of dissolved limestone grows, drying as the water evaporates.

The drop does not evaporate "on high" every time. Sometimes it falls with the dissolved limestone to the floor of the cave. But don't worry — it's not wasted. Instead of solidifying on the ceiling the limestone solidifies on the floor, and instead of growing from above it grows from below . . . . Imagine that when two such "growths" meet, a column is formed which might almost have been designed in advance to strengthen the cave.

In Soreq Cave there is a wealth of shapes. Many stalactites of various shapes reach a height of four meters. There are thread-like stalactites called erect "macaroni," cave corals, and other shapes and forms. The works of nature here surpass all imagination.

▶ A Sight at Soreq Cave

Stalactites and...Radishes at
NAHAL HAMA'AYANOT (Spring Valley)

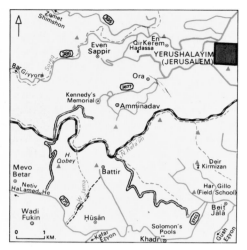

Take Road 975, the Mevo Betar–Har Gillo road. Between kilometers 19-20 there is a path between stone walls that goes down to Wadi Jama, commonly known as Nahal Hama'ayanot. You can visit one or more springs, then either go back the way you came or have someone bring the car to En Jama via Battir.

Why such a prominent photograph of radishes?

No, it is not a publicity gimmick of the Vegetable Marketing Board. But it is a recommendation to tour the valley in summer. One of the crops here is radish, which is picked, gathered, and thrown into one of the springs for washing before being taken to the village for marketing. To see a radish washed immediately after it comes out of mother earth and to taste it, even if it is not in a salad, is something special. But Nahal Hama'ayanot is beautiful and interesting even without radish. Here, land is cultivated as in the past, and there are beautiful springs and stalactite caves, and so on.

But first a description of the way down from the road. Descend towards the river. At the beginning the slope is bare and unimpressive, but a little further down, in the riverbed, there is silt, earth, springs, and irrigated agriculture. The cultivated area is divided among families in a way that is clearly visible. Sometimes you can see the farmworkers: a young girl with a spade in hand, or an old couple in their plot and beside them a young goatherd. There are more than ten springs in the river. The highest one — En Arus — the spring of the bridegroom, emerges beneath the cliff. To reach it turn off a little from the main path and pass dripping water or a soaking wet rock among ferns, moss, and maiden-hair. The dripping that becomes a run-off is collected in a reservoir and used for irrigation. A legend is told here about the beautiful Shulamit who ran away from her bridegroom (what a disgrace!). It seems that she leapt from a rock and her hair was caught on a crag. Her groom, it is said, is searching for her to this very day.

Stroll around. Water flows in ditches and is channeled to the plots by the opening and closing of the ditches. Another spring — En Hawiya — may be the spring of love. For us, however, it is the spring of radishes. Radishes and turnips and a bustle of women working. The washing of the produce seems almost like a ritual, but to the farmers it is simply work that must be finished. Down among the plots you can enter a crevice in the rock that has been widened by water. Inside is a cave. Everything drips water and round about are travertines, stalactites, and stalagmites; with a little imagination you can see all kinds of shapes and when you come out all wet, there, again, is the spring and the red of the radish.

It's worth noting: The height of the intensively cultivated plots is the same as the height of the springs where they emerge. Above this everything is less green and is supplied by rainwater and cultivated accordingly.

We have skipped over several springs but we mustn't forget En Jama. This is the spring that gave its name to the entire river. It is also the largest pool, sometimes full and sometimes disappointingly empty. The source of the water is in a spring that has been enclosed in a concrete structure at the side of the pool.

▲
Battir, the village next to the route

▶ Washing radishes in one of the springs at Nahal Hama'ayanot

Water from the Desert to Jerusalem at
EN PERAT (Ein Fara)

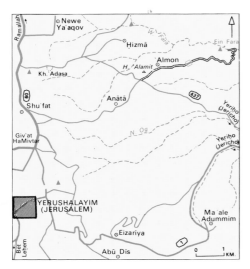

Road 437 connects Road 60, the Jerusalem–Ramallah Road, with Road 1, the Ma'ale Adummim Road. On this road, near Hirbet Alamit (which can also be reached from Jerusalem through Anata) there is a turnoff to Ein Fara, and to the new settlement Almon which is on the road going down to the spring.

Next to the turnoff to the spring is Hirbet Alamit, which some identify with the biblical town Almon, which was in the land of the tribe of Benjamin. Beside it is the grave of Sheikh Abed A-Salem.

Bypass Almon and after some 2.5 kilometers you will reach buildings that once served as a pumping station. From here a narrow desert road goes down to the riverbed and there are remains of another pumping station. It seems strange, but it is a case of desert water irrigating inhabited land . . . . From here spring water was drawn to Jerusalem with the help of a pumping station. The pumping station of En Perat also served the other springs in Nahal Perat: Qilt Spring and Ein El-Fawwar. The water was drawn upstream and from here to Jerusalem by the power of the strong pumps.

Nahal Perat, also known as Wadi Qilt, has several names, in the Arab fashion, and the section going down east from here has the name Wadi Fara, like the name of the spring, until it comes to Ein El-Fawwar and Ein Qilt and again changes names! Today, thanks to the spring that changed its name to En Perat, in Hebrew most of the river is called Nahal Perat. This is the river where Jeremiah hid a linen girdle in a cleft in the rock, as mentioned in the Book of Jeremiah 13:4. Beside the spring on a hillock is Hurvat Ein Fara. There are some who have tried to identify it as HaParah, a town belonging to the tribe of Benjamin.

The spring is some 300 meters above sea level, and from here water was not only pushed uphill to Jerusalem but in most periods going back to antiquity, water was channeled in aqueducts to fortifications and agricultural plots around the Jordan Valley. The remains of several ancient aqueducts can be found near here. Some of them are described by the Survey of Palestine, which came through here and made records in the nineteenth century. The remains of the aqueducts can be seen on both north and south banks of the river, near the spring, and downstream.

Today the spring is roofed and a large part of its past has been blurred. The aqueduct that led to a flour mill near the path can be clearly seen. Walk a little way along beside the aqueduct to the ruined mill house. From the mill and the spring walk a few steps and climb the path leading to a fenced yard with some trees. After getting permission, go to the monastery and to the few structures beside it.

At the end of the third century the first hermit monks, among them Cheriton, lived in the caves above Ein Fara. In the early fourth century, Cheriton built a church here, dedicated to Makarios, the Bishop of Jerusalem. He also established other monasteries in the Judean Desert, and at the end of his life he returned here. For a time the monastery here was called Faran, sounding like its Arabic name. On the southern cliff of the riverbed the remains of two other monasteries can be seen.

These ancient monasteries were destroyed in 614, the year when many other monasteries in the country were attacked in the brief Persian conquest. In the nineteenth century the monastery was restored and repeopled. It was abandoned again after the Six Day War, but repopulated by the church. Sometimes you will meet a monk here.

If you came in through the gate it's worth walking round the yard a little and going to the monastery on the mountainside — the one with visible rooms and windows. It is a structure hewn into the hillside. The ascent is by steps and by a ladder standing at the entrance on the terraced hill. From above you can see the rocky landscape of the river, cliffs, and patches of green beside the spring.

▲
The monastery at En Perat

▶ A view of the cliff monastery at En Perat

Aqueducts, a Waterfall, and Water at
EN QILT

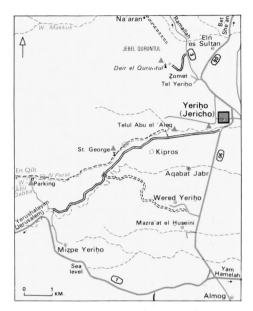

From Road 1, the Jerusalem–Jericho Road, turn off between kilometers 84–85 (22-23) to the old Jerusalem–Jericho Road, and turn onto a narrow, steep road that goes down to the carpark above the old pumphouse. From here there is a clear path to En Qilt.

▲
Winter bathing at the En Qilt Waterfall

First, where do the names Nahal Perat and Wadi Qilt come from?

As already mentioned previously, the upper section of the river bears several names, as is the Arab custom with almost every river. For most rivers the government Names Committee decided on one name for their entire length. Nahal Perat, which begins to drain at the watershed between Geva and Michmash, still has several names: Wadi Zarik, Wadi el-Hafi, Wadi Abu-Latia, Wadi-a-Radida. It is better known by the names of its springs: Wadi Fara, Wadi el-Fawwar, Wadi el-Qilt. Today it is called Nahal Perat after its highest spring, Ein Fara, which is En Perat.

We once joined a guided tour in the area. Before going down the path crossing a deep gorge, the guide read these verses from the First Book of Samuel 13:17: "And the spoilers came out of the camp of the Philistines in three companies: one company turned unto the way that leadeth to Ofrah, unto the land of Shual. And another company turned the way to Bet Horon: and another company turned to the way of the border that looketh to the valley of Zeboim toward the wilderness." When he had finished he pointed and said: This is it! We'll go down after the Philistines to the valley of hyenas called in Arabic Wadi Abu Dabba. We went down. We found neither Philistines nor hyenas (*zeboim* in Hebrew) but a huge bridge rising above us, which was actually part of the ancient aqueduct.

In the past the aqueduct brought the water from the Perat Springs to the fortress at Cyprus (near Jericho) and was used to irrigate the Jordan Valley. Apparently the first aqueducts were constructed in the Hellenistic period. Through the years further foundations were laid and sometimes additional aqueducts were built. In some of them clay pipes were laid and tunnels were even dug to take them across the hills. Sections of ancient aqueducts have remained standing along the entire length of the river, but the structure at Wadi Abu Dabba is the most impressive.

From Wadi Abu Dabba a path goes along the southern bank, and after walking for about 15 minutes you will be in the En Qilt Canyon. On the southern bank of the river in a cleft in the rock at a height of about 2 meters there is an Arabic inscription that tells of the restoration of the aqueduct in the present century. This is what it says: "In the name of the merciful and compassionate God many hundreds of years passed and the waters of the Wadi were wasted until God's inspiration came to the genius Mr. Mehia A-Din Mustapha Hillali El-Husseini. In the year 1297 of the hegira he built the dam and erected the mill and revived the gardens around them, and in 1330 of the hegira he built the channel, through which water passes to the fields of Aqabat Jabr, which is south of the town of Jericho." And indeed this aqueduct is active and carries water to Jericho to this day.

Here, take off your shoes and walk inside the canyon, against the current, to the well-known Wadi Qilt waterfall. The En Qilt spring is beside the waterfall, but the waterfall is simply the fall of water from the aqueduct coming from Ein el-Fawwar, the spring that is higher up the river.

Take a different route back to the carpark: Climb up onto the aqueduct (marked in red) ▭ and walk carefully beside it and sometimes on it or in it. Before reaching the building with the palm trees go back down to the river course. The building once served as a flour mill; today it is inhabited.

Remember, a dip in Wadi Qilt is a treat. In winter, when it's cold up on the mountain, it's warm down here. In summer, when it's hot in the desert, it's cool here. An upside down world!

► Entrance to the Wadi Qilt Canyon

A Monastery "For Men Only" at
MAR SABA

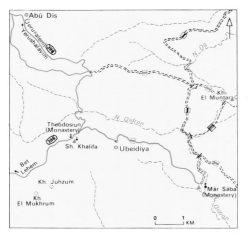

Near Road 1, the Jericho–Jerusalem Road, Road 398 connects Abu Dis with Beit Sahur, which neighbors on Bethlehem. On this road, about halfway between Beit Sahur and Abu Dis, a road turns east to the Bedouin village Ubeidiya and continues to the monastery of Mar Saba. You can also come from Beit Sahur and return via Abu Dis.

▲
A view of Mar Saba from Nahal Qidron

It's embarrassing to say but women won't be able to enter the monastery. For over 400 years no woman has crossed the threshold, and there are no indications that the monks are about to change the custom. Nevertheless, it's worth a visit, and there is a special tower for women alongside.

Around the monastery a path goes down to Nahal Qidron and up, rather steeply but not too steeply, to the road on the other side. A walk on this path is a unique experience. From here the monastery may be seen in all its strength, looking as though it is growing right out of the hillside. Just a little effort and about a 45-minute leisurely walk, and the whole panorama is yours. Furthermore, men who go into the monastery and don't follow the women down, or go down with them, will miss out.

The story of Mar Saba is permitted to both sexes. The special character of the Judean Desert made it, in various periods of history, a place of sanctuary from the law, from hostile rulers, or just from society. The relatively short distance between the desert and population centers made it at once a place far from and near to the centers of Christianity in Bethlehem and Jerusalem. At the beginning of the Anchorite movement, some monks found places of seclusion as hermits in caves in the desert cliffs. One of these early monks was Mar Saba. He was born in 439 C.E. in Cappedokia, in Asia Minor and came to live in a cave at Nahal Qidron. In the course of time other monks were drawn here and the population of cave-dwellers grew. With the growth of the population of monks the Anchorite customs changed slightly and the great monastery was built here. Mar Saba himself moved several times, both during his life and after his death. His bones were moved to Constantinople and from there they were taken to Venice. Less than twenty years ago they were returned with honor to the monastery.

The entrance to Mar Saba is through a small iron gate next to the carpark. On entering you will find yourself in a little village. Narrow lanes lead between buildings stuck to the hillside. The monastery is five storeys high and contains over 100 rooms. Today only a few monks live in this huge structure. But the monastery has seen better days. In the Byzantine period hundreds lived and entertained themselves here (if you can call this entertainment). The monastery church was established at the beginning of the sixth century, and underwent many repairs, the last time at the beginning of the nineteenth century, with financial support sent to the monks from Russia. Its position in the heart of the desert dictated its special form — like a fortress with towers. Although it was first and foremost a monastery, security problems were not unknown. In this fortress you can follow a route extending from the Byzantine church to the monks' quarters to the rear courtyard and to . . . the hall of skulls. This room resembles the hall of skulls in St. Catherine's monastery in Sinai (but there are far fewer skulls). Here, too, they separated the bones of the monks and arranged them in exemplary order. The monks claim that these are the skulls of monks who were slaughtered by the Persians during the invasion of Palestine at the beginning of the seventh century. On one of the balconies, among the trees, there is one tree that, according to tradition, was planted by Mar Saba himself.

And finally — visit the monastery of St. Theodosius (Dir Dosi), next to where the road turns off from the main road you came down to Mar Saba. Both men and women are permitted to enter this monastery.

▶ General view of Mar Saba

History, Scenery, and Cliffs at
NAHAL DARGA (Murabba'at)

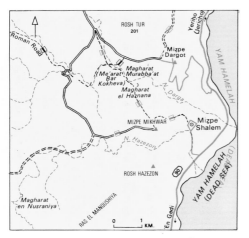

On Road 90, the road that skirts the shore of Yam Hamelah (the Dead Sea), between kilometers 258-259, a narrow road goes up to the place that was once Mizpe Shalem and which is today a touring center called Matzukei Dargot (Dargot Cliffs). The bends in the road are look-out posts in themselves. But don't stop. Go to the top, catch your breath, and look at the view. Go a little further west on a dirt road and after a kilometer or so turn south over the cliffs. Be careful not to get too near to the edge!
Several paths lead over the cliffs, and one, marked in black ▬, leads to a cave in the steep cliff. Round about are several gravestones of hikers who lost their lives here! Please be careful!!!

▲
On the way to the Bar Kokheva Caves

The name Murabba'at is what made this nahal famous and it is just this point that made it difficult for us to find it. The Arabs called it Daraja, and the Hebrew name Nahal Darga comes from this. The other sections were better known by name, while Murabba'at was the private name by which it was known to the Bedouins. On coming here after the Six Day War, we searched and searched, walked on the cliffs, went down to the river bed and didn't know that this section was Wadi Murabba'at.

The nahal is a challenge to hikers. The descent down the narrow canyon to the Dead Sea Valley with its falls, involves climbing and swimming in waterholes — and all this must be done *with* the help of a guide who knows the area and has suitable equipment. But the view from above is also impressive. And if you go down to the Bar Kokheva Cave — it will be an unforgettable experience.

Yes, Bar Kokheva.

For many years we didn't know the exact name of the man and we deliberated over the question of whether Bar Kokheva was merely a nickname. Here in this cave in 1952 documents were found — Hebrew inscriptions from the time of the Bar Kokheva revolt (132-135 C.E.), some of them signed by "Simeon son of Kosiba Prince of Israel." The name, so it is assumed today, is the name of his birthplace or the place where he lived in Khirbet Kosiba identified as being on Mount Hebron, between Hebron and Jerusalem. The letters found here, like others, were first brought out of the desert by the Bedouin tribe, Taamara, whose people have become "archaeologists." They learned the value of finds, and dug and burrowed in the caves of the Judean Desert. In order to earn more money they cut up and divided letters and scrolls into many pieces — the more the better. They sold the big and little pieces to many people and made a lot of money.

Among the letters that were found in the cave at Wadi Murabba'at were those signed by Simeon son of Kosiba and addressed to Yeshua Ben-Galgula, who was seemingly one of the commanders of Bar Kokheva's army. This commander was possibly stationed in Herodion, and apparently he fled to the cave with his people when Herodion was captured by the Romans. Here they received some of their mail and the orders of the supreme commander — Bar Kokheva. In one of the letters Bar Kokheva warns them that if his orders are not carried out he will arrest Ben-Galgula and his people, and in another he discusses a delivery of grain.

The discoveries here along with letters and documents that were unearthed later in other caves in the Judean Desert have cast important historical light on the Bar Kokheva revolt. The Romans finally made their way here and laid siege to the cave. And according to the finds, Roman soldiers went on living here even after they suppressed the revolt.

▶ A view of Nahal Darga

A Unique Oasis at
EN GEDI

Road 90 spans the entire length of Yam Hamelah (the Dead Sea). Between kilometers 244-245 there is a turnoff to the En Gedi Reserve. There are many signs at the entrance; you can't miss it.

The Nature Reserves Authority leaflet states: "En Gedi is a unique oasis noted even in the list of the world's special Nature Reserves published by the United Nations." The uniqueness of the oasis was felt more before the access road was built. In those days, in order to reach En Gedi one had to walk through the Judean Desert for several days. After this long trek in the desert seeing greenery and flowing water made one really feel the meaning of an oasis. Today there are kiosks and a youth hostel, a field school and a kibbutz, and easy access on a good road — but even so it is still an oasis, and a beautiful one.

There is much to see in the En Gedi Reserve and the Nahal Dawid route is only part of it. Our tour is a tour of the lowest level of Nahal Dawid, a signposted route suitable for everyone — about an hour-and-a-half hike. Various animals and plants of tropical origin exist here side by side with typical desert flora. In addition to the palm groves at the entrance there are the Apple of Sodom, with its hollow fruit, and the moringa, which reaches no further north than this anywhere in the world. Near them is the Christ thorn and other trees that exploit this comfortable "neighborhood." The silence enjoyed by the animals in the reserve creates surprises. You will be able to pass very close to hyraxes who have come out to graze or sunbathe. In summer it's almost impossible not to meet ibexes. A wild goat observatory has been set up at the side of the path and the animals come to within arm's length of visitors — often so near that it's hard to photograph them....

And where does the water come from? It is rainwater that comes down the high Judean Hills in the west. Some reaches the desert region as floods, permeates the surface, and flows over a subterranean level until it emerges here as springs.

Four springs make this a unique oasis. The smallest, which gave its name to the oasis, emerges high up the slope above the cultivated areas. Near it are the remains of a flour mill, indicating that here, too, in the desert, people exploited the power of the water for milling. Nahal Arugot Spring emerges in the south. Above Nahal Dawid is another small spring, En Shulamit, and of course the Dawid Springs. Over the years Nahal Dawid and Nahal Arugot "worked," preparing the soil. Huge amounts of silt were swept here from the hills. The fresh water washed part of the saline earth. The climatic conditions, the washed soil, and the water formed suitable conditions for early ripening of crops, and indeed the place was an agricultural settlement thousands of years ago. The stone tools and early structures found in the area are evidence of this. On the hill near En Gedi a Chalcolithic temple 6,000 years old has been unearthed. Saul pursued David near here, and during the Second Temple the Essenes, that sect with its own special way of life, apparently lived here. There was also a permanent settlement here, as scrolls from the Bar Kokheva period testify.

During recent centuries En Gedi was populated mainly by Bedouins. In 1953 an army settlement was established here, and later a kibbutz.

Go through a gate to the path at Nahal Dawid and follow the signs. When the path divides take the right fork. Small falls, steps, dense patches of cane, and you will arrive at the large Nahal Dawid waterfall with the cave beside it. Return via the path or on the other bank.

This, as we said, is just a mini tour. There is also Nahal Arugot, the Dodim cave, the Yavesh (or dry) waterfall, and more.

▲
Cave mouths at Nahal Dawid where finds were discovered

▶ The Dawid Waterfall at Nahal Dawid

"Fiords" at
NAHAL ZOHAR and ZOHAR FORT

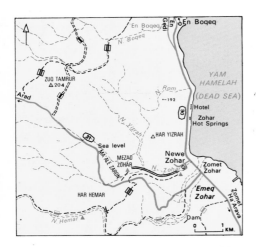

On Road 31, from Arad to Yam Hamelah (the Dead Sea), between kilometers 70-71 there are observation posts overlooking the Dead Sea, Nahal Zohar, and Mezad Zohar (Zohar Fort). Between kilometers 69-70 a path marked in green goes down to the Zohar Fort. On this path you can drive or walk through Nahal Zohar canyon to the Dead Sea shore and Newe Zohar.

What a pity we got here a "few years" late — in geological terms, that is — because if we had arrived in time we would have been able to stand here above the "Jordan Lake" that filled the Jordan Valley from around Hazeva to the Sea of Galilee. A real sea! When this sea shrank it left the Sea of Galilee, the Dead Sea, and a thread connecting them, namely the Jordan. In addition to the lakes and the river, the inland sea also left behind sediment that settled in it throughout the years, and this indicates its exact borders. For example, the light-colored brittle rock that encircles the river is lissan marl that settled in the early lake. The entire Dead Sea inlet is formed of this marl. With a little imagination you can picture the white of the marl in the water in which it settled, and come up with what is "almost" a fiord with blue bays.

In the gorge below stand the remains of a Roman-Byzantine fort. Here one of the ancient roads going down towards the Arad Valley passed the skirts of the Judean Desert and its cliffs. The road made use of the Nahal Zohar as an outlet to the Dead Sea shore. The fort stands on a hill formed of lissan marl. If you look carefully you can distinguish small dams built in the inlets of the streams to collect drinking water. You can also see a waterhole and pillars — like structures that nature carved in the soft marl. Further on down there are remains of a fortress from the Israelite Kings period, and beside them remains from the Hasmonean period. Obviously, a road passed here in those days, too. The name Zohar is found in several sites in the region: Nahal Zohar, Mezad (Fort) Zohar, and up the hill Mizpe Zohar and Rosh Zohar. In Arabic the name is Zuweira. There are some for whom the names Ras Zuweira or Kasar Zuweira (that is Zohar Fort) have more meaning.

One of the first access roads to accommodate modern vehicles in the Judean Desert was from Ras Zuweira, Rosh Zohar, uphill south of Arad towards the Dead Sea, through the course of the nahal and the fort. It was a difficult, steep road that only jeeps and special vehicles could negotiate. It served the first explorers of the region, the people of the Science Corps of the IDF of those days: Remains of the jeep road are visible up the river above the fort. When the Arad–Sedom Road was asphalted parts of the dirt road were destroyed and it is no longer in use.

Today a wide dirt road leads from Newe Zohar to the foot of the fort, but it is worth walking round the riverbed on foot. In the first section, eastward from the fort, there are many acacia trees, and further on there are canyons.

▲
Zohar Fort — a view from the east

▶ **A view of the Zohar Fort Valley from the road**

"Plug of Salt" at
HAR SEDOM

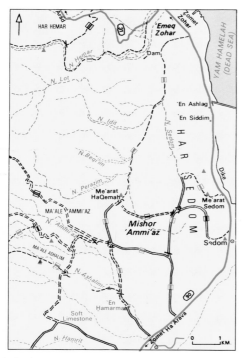

The lowest point in the world is on the Yam Hamelah (Dead Sea) shore. Begin your tour on Road 90, between kilometers 196-197 on the En Gedi–Sedom road. On the side of the road a sign marks the beginning of the Ladder Trail. Park here at the roadside, climb up, take a look round, and come back down. If there is someone to bring the car back to your starting place, continue south on Road 90 and turn off between kilometers 193-194. Follow the red sign ▭ to the Ammi'az Plain. At the first junction continue on, following the blue sign ▭ and after about 2 killometers turn right at the black sign ▬. Here at the end of the road continue on foot, while your driver returns to the Ladder Trail. Look around and go down to the Sedom Road near the beginning of the ascent to the Ladder Trail. Both the ascent and the descent are steep. Some people might find them difficult. Be careful!

Recommended time: late afternoon.

▶
Before there was a road nere: a view of Mount Sedom from the north

And all this, for what? Scenery, scenery, and more scenery. It's really something special.

First about the mountain you're climbing. Its name is Mount Sedom. The whole mountain which rises from what was once the southern Dead Sea is in fact . . . a salt plug. Simply a huge heap of salt. In fact this is in geological terms "a displacement block" which was raised above its surroundings. In order to recapitulate how the mountain rose we have to go back several million years. At that time there was a deep lake here and large amounts of sediment flowed into it from the streams. Later (as evidenced by the finds and by geological surveys) the upheaval of the block began. It rose and was immediately attacked by winds and rain, causing havoc and flattening it again. We won't bore you with the biography of the mountain and everything that happened to it — the story is long and the geological "troubles" many. But to get to the end of the story — as a result of internal shocks deep in the earth the upheaval occurred and the mountain was formed. In the ancient lake that was here, at first a layer of salt was formed and on it a stratum of heavier material. The heavy layer pressed down on the salt layer beneath it. When cracks formed in the "hard cover" the salt began to compress and rise upward. The salt rose — and the rainwater and humidity dissolved it and the contest went on. Who would get the upper hand? Meanwhile the water performed "miracles and wonders," creating statues and palaces in the easily dissolved salt — that, or returning to dissolve deep in the mountain where it formed deep shafts which hikers on the peak of Mount Sedom avoid like the plague . . . .

Mount Sedom is 11 kilometers long, 2-3 kilometers wide, and over 230 meters above sea level. If you want to go more deeply into the story of the mountain, you will find that it has caves, other paths, and of course . . . Lot's wife. You have to look for her in one of the rocks that stands out — each according to his imagination (although there are experts who point at her in a crag of salt rock above the mouth of the Sedom Cave, about 1½ kilometers north of the Ladder Trail).

▶ In one of the mountain clefts

A Robbers' Route at
NAHAL PERAZIM

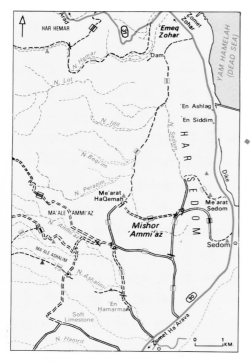

Drive along Road 90 between Yam Hamelah (the Dead Sea) and Mount Sedom, and between kilometers 193-194 turn onto a dirt road marked in red ▦ which goes up to the Ammi'az Plain. From here continue following the red markers and the signs to the river.

▲
Climbing from the Flour Cave

Before man's intervention in the works of creation the waters of the Dead Sea lapped at the foot of Mount Sedom and left no room for passage. We know of the blocked path from the stories of the late nineteenth-century explorers Blankhorne and Palmer who tried to pass by the foot of the mountain but did not succeed; they sent their party by a roundabout route, through Wadi Nuchbar Elba'al or Wadi Nechabir (for a while it was called Nahal Pitulin, the curving river bed, today called Nahal Perazim) — a narrow gorge swarming with robbers and dangerous to pass through. Today this riverbed has become a very popular tourist site and is one of the most beautiful in the Dead Sea area.

Now we do from choice what was once done for lack of it — we veer towards Nahal Perazim. From a distance it's quite difficult to distinguish the gorges of the river. When you reach the Ammi'az Plain, try to find your target. Although the gorges enclosed in high walls are near — you will not find the riverbed. This is part of its charm. Because of the danger of arriving at the wrong gorge going in the wrong direction, don't take short cuts! If you proceed following the signs everything will be all right.

Nahal Perazim is slightly different from its neighbors. The general direction of its flow is from south to north. North of Mount Sedom it joins the mouth of other riverbeds and makes its way through the brittle lissan marl, creating variegated forms — the more developed the imagination the greater the pleasure from the figures that appear along the way. Because of the small amount of rainfall in the area, the steep river banks are well preserved.

As you enter the riverbed the plain at once disappears from view and you will feel as though you are at the bottom of the world. On the walls opposite are interesting "drawings" — as if someone had engraved beautiful wall decorations at varying heights. These drawings are, apparently, the record of water currents that were formed in the shallow lake in which the marl once settled, or perhaps they are a result of the sliding and wrinkling of the soft rock, which was an outcome of the swelling of the delicate gypsum layers, leading to a shifting of the layers around them. Even if there is still disagreement concerning the source of these "drawings" no one will dispute their beauty. And as you continue along the path leaving them behind, enjoy the changing hues in the delicate layers of the river banks.

As you go deeper into the riverbed its walls lean forward. Stop after walking about 15 minutes, at the sign to the "Flour Cave." The name derives from crumbling material that sticks to the clothing of hikers, who emerge from it as white as if they had passed through a flour sack .... Go into the tunnel with a flashlight and step carefully. After a few minutes you will see light — you will be at the end of the tunnel. Here, you will climb a steep ascent, but one which is certainly negotiable. After a bit of crawling you will suddenly find yourself again on the Ammi'az Plain. Look around — where are the beautiful canyons that you walked through? If you walk about 100 meters west from the "chimney" you climbed through you will find yourself again at Nahal Perazim — this time above.

You will see your car in the distance. Return to it along the bank of the riverbed that keeps disappearing from sight.

The Euphrates Poplar at
EN HAMARMAR

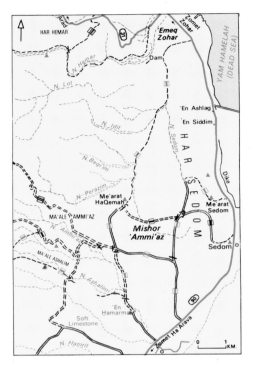

Turn-off from Road 90 south of Mount Sedom at kilometers 192-193 to Nahal Ashalim. Here a dirt road in the riverbed leads to En Hamarmar. The vegetation and the springs are about 1.5 kilometers from the road. You can also arrive upstream from the Ammi'az Plain or from the upper part of Nahal Ashalim.

If you say you have toured Nahal Ashalim people might think you have passed through its upper and middle parts, where there is a section with canyons and a large waterfall. This is a tour that takes many hours, and therefore is not on our itinerary. Our tour will take us only to the lower part.

The riverbed appears under different names on various maps — Wadi Um-Trifa, and sometimes in its lower part Wadi Halil. It begins near the factories at the edge of the Rotem Plain and ends in the area next to the evaporation ponds; once, in the good old days, it spilled into the Dead Sea. Its course and its surroundings have been ruined by roads and other modern activities, but it still has something: It has a small oasis (although no good drinking water . . .). It can hardly be compared with the oases in the Sinai Desert, but how many places are there in the desert that have a little water and a few palm trees that were not planted by man and that do not serve as a hotel garden or something of that kind . . . .

In pre-State days, the people of the Palmach (the elite underground units) passed by here on their treks. A trek of many days in the desert and the lack of potable water sometimes irritated them. Here is one description of those treks after passing through Nahal Perazim between the white marl walls: "And from here all at once a completely different landscape, a majestic sight for the wildest imagination, and again the dark wall of the hills of the Judean Desert. Afterwards the suddenness of En Hemar [Hamarmar], with its palm trees and stinking water, but cool and flowing, actually flowing . . . ."

Not always does the water actually flow, and the wide path in the riverbed diminishes in glory. But there is compensation: In the lower spring there are several palm trees and reeds — a green spot next to the Dead Sea coast. A bit further upstream is another spring, and also a cluster of Euphrates poplars — rare in this area and usually seen only near real streams of water.

All around are rocks in various shapes; some people claim to see a dog's head while others see according to their own imagination.

▲
A view of the upper spring

▶ En Hamarmar — the spring

NEGEV

The southern part of Israel, not including the area of the Elat Hills, is roughly half of the total area of the country, but its population is relatively small. When modern settlement of the country began it stopped short north of the Negev. In the settlement projects that just preceded the rise of the State, about 20 communities were established in the Negev, primarily in the northern Negev. Gevulot, Revivim, Bet Eshel — the first settlements that arose as agricultural observation stations — were then considered to be at the end of the earth. The sparse population of the south made defense of the country more difficult during the War of Independence, and there were even discussions of possibly severing parts of it from the new State of Israel. Even after the reinforcement of the Negev with settlements, the Negev mountains remained almost unpopulated due to natural conditions. Even today, Yeroham, Sede Boqer and Mizpe Ramon remain isolated along the central axis of the Negev.

In the north and west of the Negev there are remains of ancient settlement; their scale is impressive considering the desert conditions. There were agricultural farms, water collection and irrigation systems, terracing for plant cultivation and a number of towns that grew from way-stations into real cities. Archaeologists still have lots of work ahead of them in unearthing Negev cities. They have begun and are continuing to expose the secrets of Rehovot, Haluza, Nizzana and Shivta. Many hikers are familiar with the towns that have been unearthed, some of whose buildings have been reconstructed, such as Mamshit and Avedat. The special landscape of the craters also belongs to the Negev; in and around them are natural treasures that are partially exploited. To the south of the Negev mountains there were scarcely any settlements nor are there any today.

With the new deployment of the Israel Defense Forces following the peace treaty with Egypt and the withdrawal from Sinai, something changed in the southern Negev. Borot Loz or Mount Saggi, which were once inaccessible, are now connected by asphalt road. Army camps have taken over the Negev, leaving civilians little of its large area. We are lucky that the few springs, canyons and peaks in the Negev are mostly in Nahal Zin where civilians can still hike.

The Story of the Fighting Negev at the
NEGEV MONUMENT

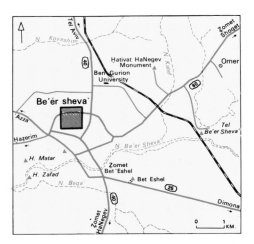

Less than 4 kilometers north-east of Be'er Sheva, between kilometers 3-4, on Road 60, the Be'er Sheva–Hebron Road, a road leads up to the Negev Brigade Monument on a hillock overlooking Be'er Sheva.

It is said of the Palmach (pre-State underground) Negev Brigade that some members are to this day embarrassed about their army ID number. While they sat under siege in the Negev, up north, army ID numbers were being given out to recruits. When the brigade came north during the cease-fire the first numbers had already been taken. And so there are Negev Brigade Palmach members who have as many as five digits in their ID number; and you can imagine how these veterans must have felt.

When the Negev Brigade returned north it was after many months of fighting and isolation. This journey was for reorganization and recuperation. As early as the beginning of October 1947 the Palmach had been made responsible for the Negev's security. At that time the Negev was populated by a few settlements. It was necessary to defend them and to maintain communication between them over the vast spaces. The "lifeline," namely the line which brought water to the settlements, had to be closely guarded. The brigade was a fighting force that moved throughout the Negev. On December 10, 1947 six members of a reconnaissance detail guarding the water line who had gone out to reconnoitre from Kibbutz Gevulot were killed. They deployed to help, to guard, and to make raids in the whole area. When the Arab forces invaded on May 15,1948 the settlements were attacked by the Egyptian regular army. The Palmach reinforced the settlements and fought with them shoulder to shoulder. During the second cease-fire, when they went north, the forces took in new recruits and after reorganizing went south again and took part in the big operations to liberate the Negev.

On the twentieth anniversary of the State of Israel, the fighters of the Negev Brigade got together with the people of the Negev to erect a monument which would be a testimony to the fighters and tell the story of the Negev before the invasion and of the war against the Egyptian invader. The monument was designed and built by the artist Danny Karavan and the garden around it by Avraham Karavan. It stands on a hill overlooking Be'er Sheva.

The monument is made up of several parts. The hill tells the story of the battle for the Negev. Imprinted in the cement of the wall at the entrance are lines of poetry, dedications, and excerpts from the battle log of the brigade as these were recorded when they occurred. On both sides of the wall is a tent-like structure which recalls the tents of the Palmach and a post — a concrete hill with communication trenches. Further on is another wall with fragments from a diary and mention of the water lines to the Negev for which the Palmach members were responsible. Engraved on the floor of the open square are maps of the operations in the form of battle sketches; opposite is a memorial dome engraved with the names of the fallen of the Negev Brigade, a bunker and a tower indicating the water towers in the settlements. From the top of the tower is a view of the entire region. Next to it is a structure which represents the Egyptian army that was defeated in the Negev. From above it looks like a cut snake. If you go inside the snake you will see the rays of light penetrating through the cracks to the end of its tail . . . .

In early spring many flowers bloom on the hillside, the most outstanding of them being the dark iris that grows right next to the wide dirt track leading out of the carpark.

The "tail" of the Egyptian army (interior photograph)

▶ A view of the Negev Brigade Monument

A Few Colors and Many Flowers —
THE YEROHAM IRIS

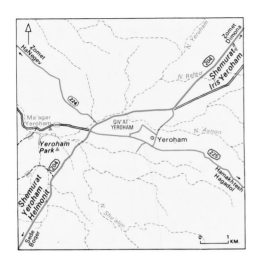

In early spring, Road 204 which joins Dimona with Yeroham, hums with activity. People are on their way to see the irises. About 4.5 kilometers from Yeroham in the direction of Dimona, between kilometers 158-159, a dirt road turns off in a general eastward direction. The Nature Reserve is about 1 kilometer from the road.

No, the large photograph does not show the characteristic color of the Yeroham iris. Perhaps we should have shown a large photograph of the more common dark iris (shown in the small photo) that is found here, but we are attracted to the unusual . . . . The dark iris is so abundant here, it's difficult to believe. So many irises and so many visitors. The pursuit of wild flowers has become a fad in Israel but fortunately the flowers are hardly affected. One of the major attractions is the iris, in all its varieties. It is certainly one of the most beautiful of all wild flowers, and can easily compete with cultivated ones.

But we haven't said much by saying, let's go and see irises. There are many species of iris in Israel, with the Gilboa iris perhaps among the most famous. The Yeroham irises we are going to see are generally more or less related to the common iris. These smaller flowers, on which we sometimes unintentionally step, are only distant relatives. Once very little was known about irises. Today they are numerous and they blossom at different times in their blossoming season. In order to enable us to visit practically all of them without discrimination they bloom at short intervals from each other, mostly in spring. We can hop from the early ones, such as the purple iris, to the Negev iris, and from it to the Nazareth iris and the Gilboa iris. We still have the Mesopotamian iris and of course — the dark Yeroham iris.

There are also iris stories. The whorled iris, for example, was painted in a book published in Europe at the end of the last century, and the readers liked it. Exporting irises became a business operation: They were brought in convoys to the ports and sent to Europe — until they became almost extinct. And there is also the opposite story of the Mesopotamian iris which came here from Iraq as a result of a Moslim custom of planting it in graveyards (it is called by some "the graveyard iris.") If you come from a northerly direction you can "catch two irises with one stone." On the slope near the Negev Brigade Monument you can see a dark iris, and here, near Yeroham, the Yeroham iris. This iris had to wait for many years until it gained its independence, that is until the existence of a Negev iris became distinct from the Yeroham iris. The dominant color in the field is purple-violet with darker shades, even brown and (fact! see the picture!) light colors beside it. The environment the Yeroham iris lives in is characteristic of the region: desert sand.

But let's not forget that there are other flowers here, too. When the irises bloom the fields are full of all kinds of blossoms. But of course the irises steal the show.

The Yeroham iris

▶ A yellow iris in the Yeroham Reserve

Boats, and Perhaps Even Fish at
LAKE YEROHAM

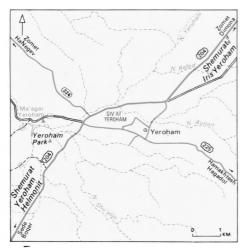

Road 204 is the road from Dimona to Sede Boqer. Between kilometers 152-151, opposite the southern entrance to Yeroham, turn onto the dirt road that goes west to Yeroham Park.

No, it's no mistake. The photograph of these trees and this blue lake are really in the Negev.

A lake set within a park, and until a few years ago one could even find Yerohamites fishing in it for carp . . . . Fishing in the desert! The story began in 1951. A transit camp for new immigrants was set up near a white hill, slightly different in color from its surroundings. The camp was called Tel Yeroham. Before the arrival of the immigrants the hill had been called Tel Rachme, and near it was a well called Bir Rachme. Like other wells in the Negev, it had been dug by the British to aid the Bedouins. There was a concrete cover over the mouth of the well and troughs were placed around it for watering the flocks. Despite the name "Tel" (mound), which usually indicates the existence of antiquities, no layers of ancient habitation were found here. In fact, Yeroham is mentioned in the writings of the Egyptian King Shishak, but remains of that period were found in a riverbed not far from here, and not on the mound.

When the first settlers came here a miners' village was planned. Its residents were meant to mine minerals in the Great Crater and its surroundings. Conditions were difficult for the immigrants. From the first settlers, immigrants from Rumania, to the permanent residents of today, there was a large turn-over. Factories were established here, including a bottling plant, a cosmetics factory, and others, to strengthen the economic base of the town. The establishment of the IDF in the Negev after the Israel-Egypt Peace Treaty brought Yeroham more into the center of things.

And the lake.

The original idea was not particularly for recreation. A dam was built on Nahal Revivim, near a narrow mountain pass, in order to collect floodwater and use it. Years have passed since then, and in rainy years water collected on the eastern side of the dam. Young carp were brought to the lake and it became a place for amateur fishermen. In summer the lake sometimes dried up completely, but in winter, when it filled up again, wonder of wonders — the fish were there again. Today the situation is bad: Many vacationers sail boats on the lake and this apparently doesn't please the fish; they simply disappear . . . .

In summer, as we said, it may be dry, and you will find perhaps just a little marsh. At the beginning of winter, in October, the sternberrings bloom in the sternberring reserve south of the lake. Then the pilgrimage of travelers turns to the southern stream and the flowers. Water, fish, boats, sternberrings — is this what they call a desert?

▲
A sternberring in bloom near the lake (October)

▶ Lake Yeroham in spring

Why People Make Pilgrimages to
SEDE BOQER

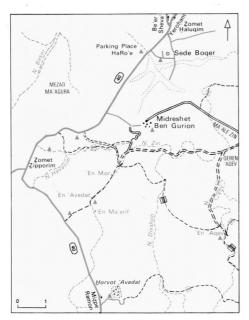

Travel south on the road from Yeroham and near Sede Boqer you will find Road 40. Or travel south from Be'er Sheva on Road 40, and south-east from Zomet Telalim (Junction). Continue on Road 40 to Sede Boqer to kilometer 134. Opposite the entrance to Ben Gurion's hut is HarRo'a Campsite. The college is 4 kilometers further on, beside kilometer 130.

▲
The graves of David and pola Ben Gurion

Once, when the Jordanian border was less than 20 kilometers from Tel Aviv, it wasn't easy to find a place as far from the border as Sede Boqer. But here, in the heart of the desert, Sede Boqer was not only far from the Jordanian border and from Egypt; in its early days it was also far from any Jewish settlement.

When the kibbutz was established in 1952, its founders hoped to make it a farm — almost a ranch, and hence — with the help of the Arabic name of the nearby hill — they decided on the name Sede Boqer, which roughly translates "Cowboy Fields." Although it was far from the border, infiltrators did reach here and attack the kibbutz. Several members were killed while working and tending flocks. HaRo'a (shepherdess') Campsite commemorates one of them, Barbara Proper, who was murdered nearby.

In developing the land, earth embankments were built to stop the floodwater, and in the large furrows that were formed fruit trees were planted. Today, the original idea of cowboys and herds has been abandoned, and the kibbutz supports itself from its orchards and field crops.

Sede Boqer received much publicity when Prime Minister David Ben Gurion resigned from office and came to settle here. He and his wife Paula lived in a modest hut. At first at his own request Ben Gurion, who was a candidate for membership of the kibbutz, worked as a shepherd. In a later period one could meet him in the early morning taking his daily walk along the main road.

Even after David Ben Gurion retired from office he remained an advisor to many in the political sphere. Sede Boqer became a place of pilgrimage and jokers called it Sede Bikur, "visitor's field." Before elections they would come to consult "the oracle in the desert," and the name Sede Boqer became Sede Bocher, "voter's field," and so on. Every event brought its own name. The soldiers of the Nahal (pioneering army corps), for example, who lived here in tents (like the veterans), called the place Sadeh BaKor, "field in the cold."

During his lifetime Ben Gurion envisaged the idea of settling the Negev and making it one of the major centers of the country. On his initiative, several educational institutions were established at a nearby campus. The institutions deal with environmental education. There is a secondary school, a branch of the Institute for Negev Research, a library, and a field school. At the entrance to the campus there is also a Gadna (youth corps) camp.

At the edge of the campus is a well-tended area with the graves of David Ben Gurion and his wife Paula. At the end of 1982 the Ben Gurion Memorial Institute was inaugurated at the entrance to the campus and the gravesite. Here the vast amount of material connected with Ben Gurion and the hundreds of thousands of documents he preserved are to be stored. The gravesite is handsomely landscaped. Along the path there is a well-tended garden and to the left and beyond it, Sede Boqer. To the right is the course of Nahal Zin, Qeren Aqev, the walls of the crater, and a lot of Negev landscape.

▶ A view of Nahal Zin

Dirt Road and "King's Highway" near
EN ZIQ

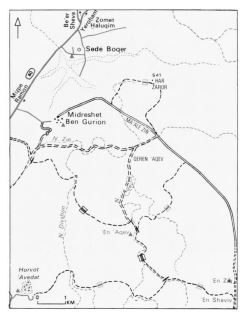

The jumping-off point here is the Sede Boqer College, which can be reached via Road 40, or Road 204 from Yeroham. From the edges of Sede Zin the trip is on dirt roads. These change after rain, floods, or other troubles. Therefore, it's a good idea to ask at the Field School at the Sede Boqer College or some other authority: a) where it is easiest to find the road leading to Ma'ale Zin; b) if it is possible to go down Ma'ale Zin and up again; c) if it is possible to cross Nahal Zin; d) the state of the road to En Zin (and, if you want to visit it, En Aqev, too); e) since there are feeding stations for animals, an observation post and a lively garbage dump, find out if the animals are in the neighborhood.

Now that you know how to get there, and everything is clear, walk along the dirt road. You are obliged to feel like a king since you are advancing along the darb A-Sultana, the king's road. "King's road" is the main road, but in some places it has become the name of a particular road. In what was once east Transjordan the name, "The King's Way," referred to the international artery connecting south and north, and similarly here in Darb A-Sultana. The road begins in the Arava Plain around En Yahav and ends at the Mediterranean Sea near Gaza. A segment of it makes use of the Nahal Zin Valley and climbs from the valley to the Zin Field Plain east of Sede Boqer at Ma'ale Zin (Nakeb Areb in Arabic). After looking at the view, go down the slope to Nahal Zin. Here go left to En Aqev, and proceed on the dirt road to En Ziq.

Where the road veers south there is a station of the oil pipeline which has left its mark on the landscape. The wide road was paved to permit access to the pipe and this nearly put an end to En Ziq. Now the spring and the oasis beside it have recovered and again there is a green patch in the desert.

The last section is easily negotiated. A few palms, perhaps a flow of water (depending on the winter rains) and you enter the green riverbed. Above are the skirts of the Avedat Heights; this is the Zinim cliff that also borders the Zin Valley which you have crossed. Ein Ziq, Ein A-Shahabia by its Arabic name, once flowed between the trees — a genuine spring flowing from beneath the roots of one of the trees in the riverbed. Stoop down and drink from the tree roots; it's a wonderful experience. Today the pleasant wood is nourished by the water of En Ziq and En Shaviv up river. The water is potable and is an interesting meeting place. At the "En Ziq Rendezvous" you can find plants and if you are lucky, animals from north and south. The most outstanding flora, in a real forest, are the Euphrates poplars. Here you can see leaves of one type on young trees, and leaves of a different kind on older trees. Should you come in summer, when it is hot and there is shade in the desert or at the end of winter when there might be a slight flow of water in the river? Perhaps the best time of all is in the fall when the poplars are shedding their leaves.

▶ En Ziq in the fall

▶
A view of En Ziq

A Canyon, and Perhaps an Ibex at
EN AVEDAT

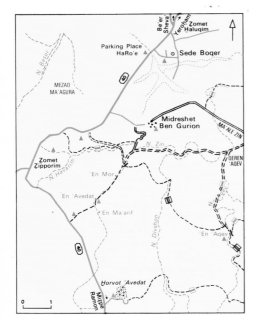

There are two ways to get to the canyon:
1) To get to the bottom of the canyon, take Road 40 from Be'er Sheva, pass Sede Boqer and turn off towards the Sede Boqer College near kilometer 130. Just before the college a wide dirt road turns off to the right and goes down to the course of Nahal Zin Riverbed and the carpark. From here proceed on foot to the En Avedat pools.
2) To get to the observation post overlooking the canyon, continue on Road 40 after passing the Sede Boqer College. About 3 kilometers before Avedat, between kilometers 124-123, turn east onto a dirt road. The carpark is about 1 kilometer from the road. From here continue on foot a few minutes until you reach the observation platform.

▲
The lower pool in the En Avedat Canyon

If you had come here years ago, the directions would have been confusing and you wouldn't have managed so well with the names. Avedat was Abdeh, and En Avedat had another name; Nahal Zin (where the spring is) was also called by a different name. True to their custom, the Arabs called the long (about 120 km) riverbed that begins near Mizpe Ramon and ends at the Dead Sea, by many different names. A traveller would have come across Wadi Nafach, Wadi Abdeh, Wadi Mura, and Wadi Fukra. Today it bears the Hebrew name of Nahal Zin along its entire length.

Millions of years ago, the course of Nahal Zin went along on flat surfaces; when it came to an area dominated by hard limestone the river cut into the rock. A sufficient amount of water (there are floodwaters here in the winter), hard limestone, and a low base into which the river flows (the Dead Sea, about 400 meters below sea level), are good conditions for the creation of a deep narrow gorge. Nahal Zin exploited these conditions.

But people don't come to the En Avedat canyon just to learn geology. Here, of course, the spring awaits us — in fact a number of springs, as well as special flora, traces of human civilization, and animals.

To begin with, prehistoric relics were found in the area, but they are not very much in evidence. Above the observation platform are remains of ancient agriculture in the form of terraces and on the cliff there are remains of a Byzantine fort (about 1,500 years old). More interesting perhaps are the caves hewn out of the western cliff of En Avedat. The approach to them is from the path descending to the spring on the "ladder ascent."

Here a number of caves which apparently served as dwellings for monks have been found including "the cave of inscriptions," the "cave of apparatus," and others without names. Among the apparatus found was a storeroom, a kitchen, and among the inscriptions one tells of St. Theodorus. The caves were probably used by the monks from nearby Avedat and their use is dated to the sixth century. Opposite the cliff of the caves, on the eastern wall, sections of a man-made tunnel were discovered and it is not clear exactly what it was used for. But there are not only remains of ancient civilization; there are views of modern life as well. From the clifftop, you can look out and see Sede Boqer College and Kibbutz Sede Boqer.

And from man to fauna. Experts and nature lovers can distinguish different kinds of birds and various rodents here. Generally speaking, whenever water is found in an area the thirsty will find their way there. If you are in luck, you will see some ibex near the water.

With regard to the flora the situation is difficult. What's the use of preparing a long list, including names such as retama, yuncus, and the like . . . ? Such a list will be of no help to ordinary hikers. So we'll begin with something big, lonely, outstanding, and easy to identify — a tree — not just any tree, but the only one in the ravine. It stands between the carpark on the path going down from Sede Boqer and the spring and it is the Atlantic pistachio. There are those who estimate it is 250 years old — and it's still worth looking at . . . .

Around the water there is the usual water flora. If you are pricked by a plant with a nail-like edge — it is the rush. The reeds can be recognized by their stalk, whereas the reedmaces have no stalk . . . And don't ignore the Euphrates poplar up river.

▶ The cliff at En Avedat

A Wayside Station that Became the City
AVEDAT

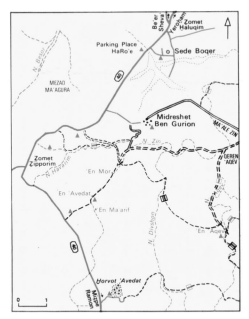

Take Road 40 to the Negev and look for Avedat near kilometer 120.

Halutza, Rehovot, Shivta, Nizana, Mamshit, and Avedat are all related. There are a few others that belong to the "Nabatean-Roman-Byzantine" family of sites, but these are the principal ones.

They all tell the story of the Negev, which was inhabited, partially cultivated, and safe for caravan movement for hundreds of years. The story is interesting, and perhaps even more so are the remains. Avedat is probably more beautiful and impressive than her relatives, and that is true of the name, as well. Nabatean Avedat was apparently named for the Nabatean King Avedat, who was worshipped as a god and buried here.

The town's story begins as a wayside station in the Hellenistic period about 2,100-2,400 years ago. On the hill the Nabateans built a town, a temple, and a pottery workshop. Later, in 106 C.E., Avedat was added to the Roman Empire. The town continued developing, additional structures were built, the acropolis (the fortified part on the hilltop) was restored or rebuilt, and a new residential area constructed. At the beginning of the fourth century Christianity reached here. Over the temple to the god Zeus one church was built, and then another. It appears that the town prospered greatly at this time — in the buildings on the ridge above and in many caves on the slope, which served as dwelling units and storage places, sometimes adjoining an exterior building. Avedat ceased to exist a short time after the Arab conquest of Palestine. In 636 the Arabs completed the conquest, the roads were neglected, security was breached, and the Negev towns, including Avedat, were abandoned. The rediscovery of Avedat is credited to the Englishman Palmer, who explored the region at the end of the last century on behalf of the Palestine Exploration Fund. Others followed him and added details. Beginning in 1958, excavations and restoration were conducted here for several seasons, and the site was prepared for visitors.

Start your visit at the upper carpark. On your way there you will pass an interesting burial cave about 100 meters from the road. Up above, near the carpark and at the edges of the Roman quarter, is the "Roman tower." Go up to the second floor and look out over the site from there. Beside the tower there is a building, and in the "main street" next to it is a water cistern and a drainage channel. A little further on, go down carefully to the "salt cave," which stored the substances used for preserving. You can lick the wall and confirm that it was really salt that was stored here. By way of the winepress go on to the fortress. The fortress has several gates, a large water cistern in its center, and a tower with steps. It's worth the climb. From the tower you can see to the end of the acropolis at the west of the site, and this is where you are heading now. Pass the southern church and go on to a vestibule with pillars that is next to a church. Apparently the vestibule was built in the Nabatean period and repaired and rebuilt later. Scattered near it are Nabatean inscriptions and on one of the pillars is a dedication to the builder.

From the vestibule go down a Nabatean staircase to the "shopping arcade." From here you can view the restored ancient farm and easily descend towards the lower carpark. Along the way are the dwelling caves, the winepresses, the storerooms, and the buildings adjoining the caves. From here, either return to the upper carpark, or with luck your car will be waiting for you down here below.

This discussion of Avedat has been very brief. One should certainly preprare for the tour so as to see as much as possible.

▲
A general view of the acropolis

▶ **The western square at Avedat**

Ponds and Desert on the Way to
BOROT LOZ (Loz Ponds)

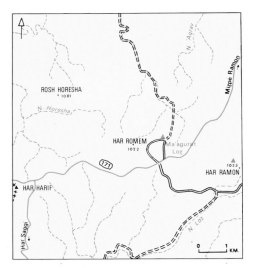

On Road 40, some 5 kilometers north of Mizpe Ramon, Road 171 branches off towards Mishor Haruchot, Har Harif, and Ma'aleh Arod. Details are on the map on page 157. About 30 kilometers from the road, before the turnoff to Ma'aleh Arod and the foot of Mount Harif, a dirt road branches off to Borot Loz (one well, named Ma'agurat Loz, is marked on the map). The path is marked. There are signposts and a dirt road which is rather difficult, but it's only one kilometer long. This is an army firing range, and if there is training and firing going on in the area, it's not worth the visit — and you won't be allowed in anyway. On week-ends and holidays the firing usually stops and the ranges are silent.

For anyone who hasn't been here in a long time, Road 171 is a surprise or a shock. Once it was the end of the world. Ma'aleh Arod could be reached only on foot or by jeep. Har Harif? Few went there. Today an asphalt road passes Har Aricha and the training areas, circumvents Mahtesh Ramon, and climbs towards Har Saggi. In summer this is a scorching, almost unbearable route. Although it is several hundred meters above sea level it is still very hot in the daytime. In winter it is cold. Whoever likes the desert will like this region. In early spring it is a blanket of wild blooms, colors, and scents.

There are hints right at the beginning of the place you are going to visit. Back at the Plain of the Winds, anyone with a sharp eye will have distinguished channels gliding down the hillside. These carry surface run-off water to pools at the foot of the hill. About seven kilometers from the Sede Boqer–Mizpe Ramon Road (Road 40) is Bor Hemet (Hemet Pond). Like in the movies — it is a "preview" of Borot Loz (Loz Ponds) to which you are heading. There are Atlantic pistachios all along the route.

The Atlantic pistachio also grows in Galilee and near Jerusalem, but it is a wonder to see this large tree here in the Negev.... The largest concentration of pistachios is at Nahal Elot and Nahal Horesha not far from here, but as mentioned, there are representatives along the way. Interestingly, most hikers are familiar with the Negev Atlantic pistachio when it is naked. In winter it stands without its foliage, dry, looking from afar like a burnt tree. But in summer it looks like a real tree, a spot of shade and green, and all around it are stones and more stones. Who knows — perhaps they are a relic of the days when more rain fell in the region?

Loz ponds are ancient. There are some who attribute them to the period of the Kings of Judah, and perhaps these are the ones mentioned in a biblical story about King Uzziah. Some of the ponds are square and up to three feet deep. They are dug in soft rock and lined with stones. Nearby are ancient structures, some of which have been excavated. There is a campsite for sleeping under the stars. The campsite is walled in for protection from the wind, and to make it possible to build a fire. From the campsite the dirt road climbs up to one of the ponds and continues to the biggest one, about 300 meters from the campsite.

In a rainy year, the ponds fill up with water and it's difficult to see how deep they are, how they are built, and the rough stones that line them.

▲
Blooms near the Ma'agura (April)

► Ma'agurat Loz (one of the ponds in the area)

How They Almost Destroyed
EN YORQE'AM (Yorqe'am Springs)

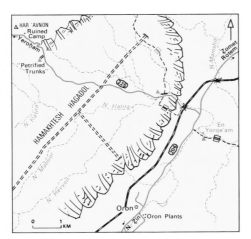

On Road 206, between Zomet Rotem (Junction) and the phosphate works, there is a sign to Nahal Yorqe'am between kilometers 17-16. You can also drive from Yeroham on Road 225, enjoy the sights of the Great Crater, and join up with Road 206 beside the signpost.

A "heap of stones" on the eastern side of the road marks the beginning of the way. If you look closely, however, you will see that this "heap" is in fact a structure with rooms, which was probably a fort. Apparently soldiers — during the Byzantine period — passed their time guarding the way south and perhaps also guarding the access to En Yorqe'am.

From the fort the path goes down to the course of Nahal Yorqe'am and after a walk of about half a kilometer you will be above a very lovely spot.

Looking down at En Yorqe'am from the cliff you will see a deep channel cut into the rock. This is the continuation of the river which begins at the crater. Some distance from the side of the crater the river course changes and moves from a region of soft rock to hard rock. At the point the soft and hard rock meet there are beautiful waterfalls and canyons, and in season waters spring forth at the base of the canyon, forming pools of rainwater and, in winter, floods.

Descend to the base of the waterfall from the northern side of the river. From above you will see a set of steps carved into the rock. These date to the time when the fort was constructed, about 1,600 years ago, and were designed to help man and beast descend to the spring and the waterholes. Inside the canyon the spring hardly flows. In summer it is mostly dry, when the only source of water is the waterholes which retain the rainwater collected in them.

There are lots of other things to look at beside the waterfall and the spring. With a little imagination you will discover various shapes and forms here when looking up at the sky, including a human head and a lion's head.

Just a little down river you will see signs of drilling in the rock, and if the story wasn't so sad we would certainly laugh at the stupidity of what was done here. A few years ago someone came up with the idea of decorating another area in the Negev with rock sculptures; the source of rock was here at En Yorqe'am. The people involved in the project evidently believed that it was justified to bring beauty to one place even at the expense of destroying another. Did they really believe there were no other rocks and stones elsewhere in the Negev?

▲
Water at En Yorqe'am

► En Yorqe'am

"Potatoes" and Sharks' Teeth at
NAHAL ZIN

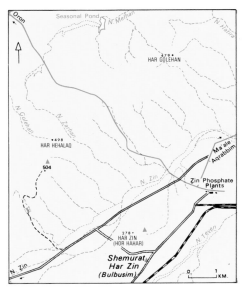

Drive on Road 206, which branches off from Road 25 at Zomet Rotem (Junction) east of Dimona, to the phosphate works. From here you will have to use the phosphate works' private road so be sure to get permission. Continue on the factory road until you reach another, newer phosphate works at Nahal Zin near Hor-Hahar, which is Mount Zin on the map. You can also come from Road 227, which branches off from Road 90, the Arava Road at En Hazeva. (See details on the map on p. 157.)

How do you find potatoes and sharks' teeth in the Negev?

Look for Hor-Hahar, which may or may not be the biblical Hor-Hahar, but it is a residual hill standing out well above its surroundings and definitely suitable to serve as a signpost. The "potato field" stretches to the south of it. All around are machinery, noise, and dust. Strata containing phosphates are found only beside the hill and the "potato field," and inside the soft clay right at the roadside there are phosphates and . . . sharks' teeth, even teeth "in good condition." Yes, there is a connection between sharks' teeth and fish and phosphates, and the connection took place millions of years ago when sharks lived in the neighborhood.

But to the potatoes. This is an extraordinary phenomenon — rounded stones that look as though they were made of two halves stuck together. There are flint potatoes elsewhere in Israel but those here are composed of limestone concretion. When the phosphate works were first set up here this field was nearly destroyed. Under pressure from various bodies and following cries of protest the field remained outside the phosphate mining area, and everyone benefited.

As to the origin of the round, potato-like, chalk stones — there are many stories, and every hiker adds his own versions . . . . One legend maintains that the Prophet Elijah passed here through a watermelon field. When he asked if he could refresh himself with watermelon, the owner refused. In his great anger Elijah turned the watermelons into stones. This legend is also told of other places in Israel, so we will look elsewhere.

The source of another legend is the Koran, which says that Allah showered stones on the people of Lot. Perhaps it all happened here at Nahal Zin. Travellers who toured the Negev in the last century heard of a town on the hilltop, all of whose inhabitants had been sinners. As punishment Allah had brought down a shower of stones on the town and its citizens — and this, according to the travellers, is the source of the stones. Another version maintains that the stones are the heads of the town's people. What about the bodies? About this they offer no explanation.

Because geologists have found no explanation for how the stones were formed, we are quoting legends and leaving lots of room for imagination.

At the edge of the potato field there was an ancient parking lot with a Greek inscription and several shards. Perhaps this was a wayside post next to the road that passed here.

Please leave the potatoes where they are. It's true there are a lot of them but there are even more hikers who want to go on enjoying the large collection as it stands. And anyway, who wants to get involved with Elijah's cursed watermelons, or with the heads of sinners?

▲
"Hor-Hahar" — Mount Zin

▶ The potato field at Nahal Zin

Green in the Oasis of
EN AQRABBIM and EN ZIN

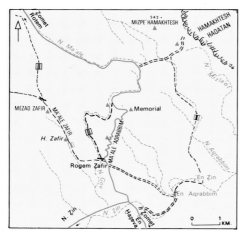

On Road 227 about 200 meters south of the foot of the pass of Ma'ale Aqrabbim (Scorpion Pass), a dirt road turns southeast on the rocky plain. This is a short cut to the campsite and to the place from the look-out point over the green course of Nahal Zin between En Aqrabbim and En Zin. From the observation point, it is possible to descend to the ravine, and to tour En Aqrabbim and En Zin.
Another dirt road branches off from Road 227 about 350 meters south of the road leading to the phosphate works at Nahal Zin and south of where Road 227 crosses the course of Nahal Zin. From here it is about 2 kilometers up the river to En Aqrabbim and another kilometer to En Zin.

The old-timers know it by name: Wadi Fukra, the long riverbed whose upper streams are near Mahtesh Ramon. If you are concerned with how long is long, then what you have here is the second longest of the Negev riverbeds, after Nahal Paran. Along the ravine are most of the Negev springs (but there are only a few of these — En Avedat, En Aqev, and En Ziq.) Here at the foot of Ma'ale Aqrabbim are the springs En Aqrabbim and En Zin, and further on craters — the famous waterholes of Nahal Zin, which become swimming pools in the desert after a flood. (Don't get excited and run! It's over 7 kilometers from here!) Nahal Zin ends its journey in the southern part of the Dead Sea and one crosses its impressive course travelling on the Arava Road south of Sedom Junction.

The beginning of the green patch you are going to see is a forest of tamarisks and prosopises. The map is marked with a blue eye, indicating water at En Aqrabbim, but to see it when there is water flowing is a rare occasion. The spring is generally dry. From here, about a kilometer down river, there is something you won't want to miss! Here, too, a blue eye is marked on the path, and this is En Zin. You'll get little satisfaction here. There is a small spring whose water you can drink if you must, but it is very bitter.

The view here is compensation for the bitterness — scores of palms creating a landscape that gives shade and provides contrast to the light color of the arid surroundings. Among the palms are tamarisks, prosopises, niterbushes, and even water-loving plants such as reedmaces, reeds, and rush.

This beautiful spot is threatened by all kinds of evil. There are some who come all the way here to strip the palms of fronds for the Feast of Tabernacles. Careless vacationers or Bedouins sometimes are responsible for fires that burn the brush.

But if your timing is right and luck is on your side you will find a little water here and perhaps meet animals coming to the spring to drink.

▶ **After a fire at En Zin**

▶
En Zin

THE HILLS OF ELAT

Although this is actually the southern Negev, it is called the hills of Elat. This region differs in character and landscape from the other parts of the Negev and, with the blue water and the under-water world of the Gulf of Elat, it is another world.

Once Elat could be reached only either by air, through the Arava that defines the Negev in the east, or via the central axis of the Negev through Mizpe Ramon and Makhtesh Ramon. Now it can also be reached from the direction of the Israel–Egypt border. Whatever the way, on approaching the region something different is discernable. Different types of rock create a changed landscape with myriad shades and colors. A story is told that some of the angels sent to paint the earth after creation neglected their task; they tired of their work while they were in the Elat area, and here they spilled all their paint — some on the hills and some in the sea. The blue — colored the water and the other colors colored the fish and the corals.

Standing out against the skyline are the craggy peaks of the hills, made of dark base rock and beside them light chalk rocks. There are also sandstone formations and when you reach these the wealth of color makes the imagination run wild. The sandstone has given us the "mushroom," Solomon's Pillars, the red canyon and other spots. The size of the region is less than a hundred square kilometers yet we have devoted about one tenth of the spots in this book to it.

In winter, spring and autumn this is simply a charming area, and nothing more need be said. In summer, there is the sea, and this is a world unto itself. We learn from the Bible that King Solomon built a fleet in Elat on the shore of the Red Sea. He built a fleet and a port but he surely did not do it as a result of the beauty of the place.

According to world experts, the sea in the Gulf of Elat and its underwater world are among the most beautiful anywhere. We'll take their word for it.

Goddess and Animals at
HAY BAR (Wildlife)

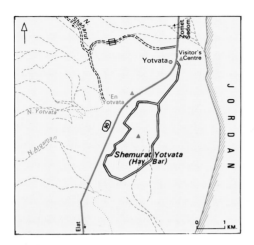

Start counting kilometer signs on Road 90, the Arava Road, after you pass Zomet Arava (Junction). When you get to kilometers 52-51, you'll be near Kibbutz Yotvata. The entrance to the Hay Bar is marked at the gas station and the visitors' center.

The Hay Bar site stole the show from Yotvata. Previously, when people passed by here or visited they might mention that perhaps this was the biblical Yotvata, one of the stations of the Children of Israel during their forty-year trek through the desert. Or they would visit the nearby remains of a fortress from the Israelite period, the later fort, the bath-house, and a chain well-system. They might discuss the similarity between the name En Ghadian and the Roman goddess of the hunt and mention there had been a wayside station here referred to on an ancient map as A-Diana and that perhaps its name had been bastardized to Ghadian? Or they might have visited the kibbutz agricultural station here. But Kibbutz Yotvata grew, built itself a cowshed, and began producing dairy products . . . and other things. Today it has a lovely tourist center. Beside it is the nature reserve, which may be turned into a national park for wild animals. They call it Hay Bar — wildlife.

The idea behind Hay Bar is to attempt to rescue Israel's wildlife and return it to its former state — at least partially. Once there were lions and leopards here (these are being rediscovered!) and ostriches and oryx. Why shouldn't they come back here to live? When the idea began to take shape work was begun fencing in thousands of acres and when the "house" was ready the tennants began to arrive. The first were old-timers in the region who had never deserted it — the gazelles. While the fences were being put up more than twenty gazelles were "accidentally" caught here, and these reproduced and there are nearly 100 today. Gradually other residents arrived. The first immigrants from abroad were the wild asses. At first glance the wild ass looks just like a donkey, but on further inspection it is quite different. It was brought here from Iran and resembles the Syrian ass that lived here in the past. But not only donkeys came to live in the reserve. Ostriches came, too, and some of them are very cheeky. When tourists come to visit they stick their long necks through every open car window and cannot resist a good wristwatch that isn't fastened properly, which they will swallow . . . .

Add to these addaxes, oryxes, ibexes, and other passers-by — some winged and some "locals" — and you will have a cross-section of the population of Hay Bar. But remember: The animals are not waiting for you in cages. Their population is sparse as befits life in the wild and there are no apartments with shared courtyards and balconies facing each other. Thus when you drive carefully through the paths of the park you won't always see all of them. Perhaps you can take consolation in the fact that you can observe or try to observe them from the observation tower, and in the knowledge that they can certainly see you.

▲
Acacias and a look at the savannah in the Arava at Hay Bar

▶ Addaxes at Hay Bar

A Mushroom and Mines in the NORTH TIMNA VALLEY

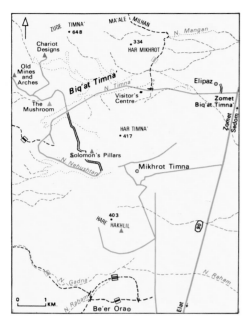

From Road 90, the Arava Road, between kilometers 38-39, a road turns west towards the Timna Valley. At the entrance is a booth where you will pay an entrance fee. Inside you can visit Solomon's Pillars, an Egyptian temple, and other sites. Everything is near the paths and well organized. It's a good idea to get a map and a guidebook at the entrance and to look over the page that deals with the South Timna Valley, too.

▲
Arches in the north Timna Valley

The "mushroom" is at the center of the valley and competed with Solomon's Pillars for the right to be the "trade mark" of the Timna Valley treasures. Like Solomon's Pillars in the southern part of the valley, the "mushroom" is made of sandstone. Decaying processes separated it from the nearby hill and formed its distinctive shape. Near the "mushroom" are remains of ancient structures — some Egyptian, some even earlier. Copper was mined here more than 6,000 years ago by local tribes, among them perhaps the members of the tribe of Tubal Cain mentioned in the Bible. Among the structures is an oven that is one of the oldest in the world — more than 5,000 years old. Shafts for mining ore, storehouses, a temple, and of course relics from copper mining were also discovered here. In Israel Timna is synonymous with copper.

The copper that was mined here in ancient times was not the same type that is mined in the new works. It appeared in high concentrates and was extracted by smelting. The concentrates were found in the white sandstone layers of an underground mine system. In the Egyptian period a system of vertical shafts was used. After mining, the concentrates were ground to powder and placed in the smelting oven. At the end of the process the drops of copper were removed from the dross. All these, the mines (some of them scores of meters deep) and other signs of processing, are to be found in the valley and you can visit them, too.

The Romans also had their place in the story of Timna. They apparently inspected the mines and left signs that they, too, had been here. There is a Roman inscription on a cave approached through one of the ravines, and getting there is an experience in itself. In another ravine an approach was made to a crevice in the rock and inside it are drawings of chariots. These are about 3,000 years old (again from the Egyption period) and some think they are even older. Among the drawings: hunters with bows and arrows, animals, including ostriches and ibex, and the most interesting of all, the drawings of chariots carrying Egyptian soldiers, in some of which the riders (perhaps) carry shields and bows. The drawings are engraved in the rock and some are even painted red and white.

The valley is constantly changing — different hours bring different landscapes. The cliffs surrounding the valley, the sphynx-like rocks (in the south), the "mushroom" and the other sites look different with the changing lights and shadows of the day. The variety of rocks found at Timna gives it its special beauty. It is encircled by cliffs with narrow ravines, relics of the past, and the dominant sandstone in various colors and shapes; your imagination is your only limitation.

An example of nature's pranks are the arches or windows in the white stone cliffs. A set of steps, put there for the convenience of climbers, brings you to the arches — which are the result of chemical decay in the sandstone. How much imagination do you need here to guess the scope of nature's creativity. Here is the reality — from every angle a different landscape can be seen.

▶ The "mushroom" at Timna Valley

A King, a Goddess, and a Snake at
SOUTH TIMNA VALLEY

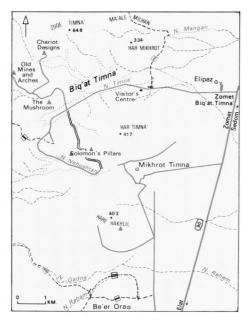

From Road 90, the Arava Road, between kilometers 38-39, a road turns west to the Timna Valley. At the entrance is a booth and . . . an entrance fee. Inside: a beautiful desert landscape. It's worth getting a map and guidebooks at the entrance booth. It's worth reading about the North Timna Valley, too.

The eastern Solomon's Pillars

The southern part of the Timna Valley is more familiar than the northern — the copper mines of Timna are here, and so are Solomon's Pillars. And who hasn't heard of Solomon's Pillars?

With regard to Solomon's Pillars, there were some disappointments. At first we had counted on what was written in the Book of Deuteronomy (8:9): "A land whose stones are iron, and out of whose hills thou mayest dig copper." When it turned out that there was copper at Timna, we connected it with the stories about King Solomon, because he was the king who opened a road to the Red Sea, made international connections, and developed the country. Thus, the large pillars, which are actually two beautiful groups of sandstone formations, were pictured in our imagination as "Solomon's Pillars," and the copper mines as "Solomon's Mines."

And the facts? The pillars, as we have known for a long time, are a creation of nature, which was greater even than Solomon . . . formed of hard sandstone. Sandstone consists of parts of quartz, granite, and grains of sand. For years water eroded the sandstone slopes and created these impressive shapes. The age of the sandstone is between 100-250 million years.

And the copper? It was first mined in ancient times, before the days of Solomon. Beside the eastern group of pillars, an Egyptian temple was discovered. When the temple was excavated it was found to be about 3,400 years old (it existed from the end of the fourteenth century B.C.E. until the middle of the twelfth century B.C.E.) and the copper smelting camps and ancient copper mines are the same age. The temple is small and statues of the goddess Hathor, an Egyptian goddess connected with mining, were found in it, as well as an altar, tools, and other items, an inscription of the kings of Egypt and . . . a copper snake with a gilded head. On a rock surface above the temple a rock painting was found, depicting one of the Egyptian kings, Ramses III, making an offering to the goddess Hathor. Obviously, an Egyptian mining expedition was here long, long ago . . . .

From the temple there is a path and a stairway built especially for the ascent to the observation platform over the valley, and also to the painting above the platform. To the east of the Egyptian temple and Solomon's Pillars is the modern Timna works. Copper used to be mined here, but following changes in the world copper market the mine was closed. Now maintenance work and other activities continue on a small scale. North of the group of Solomon's Pillars (the one next to the Egyptian temple) is another, slightly different group. You can go down to it on the path from the observation platform or walk at the foot of the cliffs.

A dirt road encircles the southern part of the valley and passes by a hill called "Slaves' Hill." When roads were prepared in the Timna Valley they were signposted and the visits "institutionalized." Sites were added that were easily accessible, even to those who are not seasoned hikers.

Endless Arava, and then
DOUM PALM

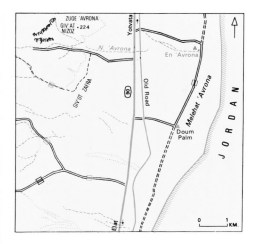

Almost at the end of the Arava Road, Road 90, at the approach to Elat, between kilometers 23-22, a short dirt road marked in black ■ turns east, leading to a group of doum palms.

Most people coming from the north are heading for Elat and this is almost the end of the road; we've come to the end of the Arraba and we've hardly said anything about it.

Well, if one arranged to "meet in the Arava," it would be quite difficult — and not because the Arava is so long but because in the Bible, for example, the name Arava refers simply to any desert area.

Nevertheless, there has been some definition with regard to Arava. If we say simply, Arava, it will refer to that part of the Syrian-African rift from the Dead Sea to the Gulf of Elat — altogether about 175 kilometers. This Arava has its eastern border in the Hills of Edom, its western one in the Negev, and it ranges in width from a few kilometers in the south to a maximum of some 25 kilometers in the north. The 175 kilometers can be divided as follows: The northern Arava stretches from the Dead Sea to as far as the Notza Range; the southern Arava stretches from the Notza Range to the Gulf of Elat. The border, the Notza Range, rises to a height of 260 meters above sea level. Think about it: from the Dead Sea, which is about 400 meters below sea level, to the Notza Range, there is a rise in elevation of about 650-660 meters. From the Notza Range to Elat — a descent. And this is how the rivers behave: Some drain northwards to the Dead Sea and some southwards to the Gulf of Elat.

There are many stories about the Arava, but we'll be brief. There were roads here in the ancient past, and fortresses. At its fringes there were several springs. But for hundreds of years the Arava stood desolate. When the borderlines in the region were fixed in consequence of a series of agreements at the end of World War I, and later upon the establishment of the Kingdom of Jordan, it was determined that the borderline would be at the lowest place in the Arava. This decision led to occasional slight changes and arguments as to what was the lowest place, since the terrain changed as a reuslt of floods and erosion or because of some other activity. The Arava was resettled during the twentieth century with the beginning of Jewish settlement; today there are several settlements along its length and others are in the planning stages.

If you rush southwards without taking time to look around, everything will seem uniform and monotonous. The road approaches the hills and moves away from them. Sometimes it crosses a riverbed. The dominant flora (as seen through the car window) consists mainly of acacias. On closer look, however, you can discern various shapes in the landscape of acacias. Sometimes you can see a parasitic plant on a tree which adds color (it's called the acacia strap flower.) Exaggerators claim that this is an African-type savannah landscape, but that is really stretching things. There are some unusual features, and one of them is the doum plam. It is different from other palms in the country. Its trunk is branched and its fruit is also different: not dates but round, hard fruit. In Africa — where this palm is common — the fruit is ground and mixed with seeds and other types of food. The uniqueness of the tree here is that it is the northernmost doum palm in the world. Its nearest relatives are at Tabah, south of Elat, beyond the new border with Egypt. To the north of the palm is a spring — En Avrona — and to its east the patrol road and the Jordanian border. Please pay attention.

▲
The well at En Avrona

▶ Doum palm in the Arava

The Magnificent Five — the Pillars at
NAHAL AMRAM

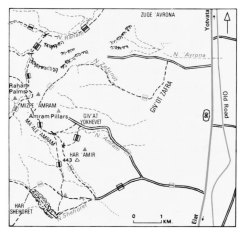

From Road 90, Arava Road, a dirt road marked in blue ▥ turns off between kilometers 20-21. This leads west and after about 2.5 kilometers it forks. Take the right fork (still marked in blue) and go on for another 5 kilometers to where the road ends in a carpark. From here, continue on foot for about five minutes to the Amram Pillars.

You will already see the variegated hues while driving west on the dirt road — dark and bright patches on the hill and craggy peaks. There is clearly *something* in store. The road leads along the course of Nahal Amram and brings you to the Amram Valley. There are those who claim it is more like a crater than a valley, and you will see this more clearly from the surrounding cliffs; it is an imperfect crater surrounded by cliffs from three sides only.

Enter through the southern fringes of the valley. On your left are the cliffs of Mount Amir and opposite, in the west, the cliffs below Mizpe Amram (which is a fantastic observation point. It has a very steep path and is quite hard to climb, but from here an entire world is at your feet!)

What does the Amram Valley have to offer?

A lot.

For example, very ancient volcanic rocks. But if the great age of the valley does not impress you, turn to the view: bare sand in shades of white and beautiful shapes. Limestones and rocks and a confusion of layers, and colors. And as if the whims of nature were not enough here, man also added a bit: On the slopes of Mount Amir and close to the Amram Pillars there are ancient mines hewn into the layers of sandstone. And whoever is not satisfied with what there is on the earth's surface — please, go inside . . . .

The largest and most ancient of the mines are atop Mount Amir, but there are also mines near the carpark at the end of the dirt road at Nahal Amram. You can reach them by going west from the carprak towards the Amram Pillars. About 200 meters from the carpark a ravine leads left. Climb, perhaps lose your way a bit, and maybe you'll find it.

The path to the Amram Pillars is clear. It passes the "Waffle" rock, a split block with layers in various shades (here, too, you can turn left to the ancient mines). The Amram Pillars are beneath the cliffs of Mizpe Amram and are part of it. Five impressive pillars were formed with the generous help of the water that attacked the cliff in cracks and crevices that had apparently been in it, and created a work of art. The pillars look beautiful from far off, from nearby, on close inspection from below, from above, and from every conceivable angle.

Make no mistake about the name. There is no connection between the biblical Amram and these pillars, the way they were formed, and the stories here. Simply, the Arabic name of the river was Wadi Amrani, and the Hebrew name merely retains the sound.

▶ The Amram Pillars

▶
The "waffle" at the entrance to the Amram Pillars

A Canyon and Small Falls at
NAHAL SHEHORET

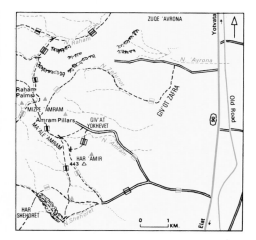

Turn off from Road 90, the Arava Road, between kilometers 20-21 onto a dirt road marked in blue ▣ . After about two and a half kilometers the road turns left and the marking is green ▣ . Three and a half kilometers further on, a rather difficult part of the dirt road leads to the mouth of Nahal Shehoret.

The green path continues into the canyon. You can go back by the same route, or continue on and tour the vicinity.

Shehoret Canyon is definitely a respectable destination. It is not a long tour — only about 1,200 meters between dark walls. If you open your eyes you can see forms of landscape, different colors in the rock surface — one big jumble.

Here, for example, at the entrance to the canyon the river cuts its course between high silt steps. It is as if pebbles and stones had been taken out and piled in layers like passage walls. And indeed, that's how it happened: In the past the river dragged silt with it and layered it here, and in the course of time it began to cut into its own bed and its course deepened inside the silt. This is clear to the eye.

But only silt steps?

It's an open secret that the rock crust in the region of Elat is unique. Here ancient rocks are exposed. Touching 600 million-year-old rock at the entrance to Shehoret is no trifling matter. These are base rocks that solidified from magmatic matter that arose from the bowels of the earth and cooled slowly. Slow cooling means large crystals. If you examine some of the stones here you will see the large and small crystals. If you don't see them — it's a sign you lifted the wrong stone! And there is also something "younger" — limestone that settled in the sea and was exposed. Around here there is clay and sandstone in different shades between layers of rock, and more. And remember — every rock surface creates a different scene, hence you are in for a spectacular show.

The green marker ▣ leads up the nahal in the canyon. Here the course of the Shehoret crosses a section of metamorphic rock. This is rock that has undergone a transformation — a metamorphosis — under the influence of heat and so forth. South of the riverbed are steep slopes and to the north a more hilly landscape. Here and there are small falls, "only" a meter or two high. With a slight effort, a push or a pull — you'll manage!

At the end of the canyon the riverbed broadens a little. Here you can discern the bright shades of the sedimentary rock beside the dark shades of the base rock. A path marked in red ▣ goes up to the south. On the fault line the line of contact between the rocks is clearly visible. Here, too, whoever isn't interested in metamorphic and sedimentary and base rocks can simply look: there are differences in color, a difference in landscape and one needn't bother with calculations of a hundred million years here or there. You can return through the canyon to the mouth of the river. The descent through the falls is easy: simply sit down and slide carefully. But it's worth following the red marker on the path ▣ which turns right and goes up to a region of sea sedimentary rock in which you can find fossils. From there go down the river course a little to a black-marked path ▣ which goes south almost to the carpark.

The branch of the river coming down from Mount Amir, which stands out to the North is called north Nahal Shehoret, and has a marked path (it is the continuation of the black path ▣ on which you descended to the car, but with a turnoff to the north, that is, left). This is a very lovely section with sandstone, variegated shapes, niches in the rock, and an example of what sandstone can offer.

▲
At north Nahal Shehoret

▶ Emerging from the canyon

A Descent through a Narrow Cleft at
EN NETAFIM

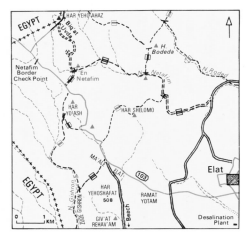

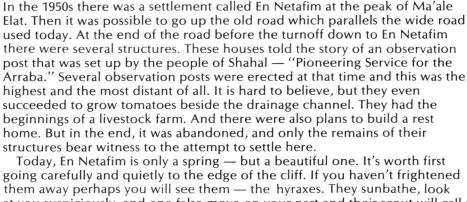

From Elat travel on Road 103 towards Ma'ale Elat. A little after the end of the pass, follow the signs on a steep dirt road. This is a section that was once an Israeli patrol road along the border; it goes down to the carpark at a distance of less than a kilometer from the road just above the cliff of En Netafim. From the carpark a path marked in green ▣ goes down to the spring.

In the 1950s there was a settlement called En Netafim at the peak of Ma'ale Elat. Then it was possible to go up the old road which parallels the wide road used today. At the end of the road before the turnoff down to En Netafim there were several structures. These houses told the story of an observation post that was set up by the people of Shahal — "Pioneering Service for the Arraba." Several observation posts were erected at that time and this was the highest and the most distant of all. It is hard to believe, but they even succeeded to grow tomatoes beside the drainage channel. They had the beginnings of a livestock farm. And there were also plans to build a rest home. But in the end, it was abandoned, and only the remains of their structures bear witness to the attempt to settle here.

Today, En Netafim is only a spring — but a beautiful one. It's worth first going carefully and quietly to the edge of the cliff. If you haven't frightened them away perhaps you will see them — the hyraxes. They sunbathe, look at you suspiciously, and one false move on your part and their scout will call a warning; they will all disappear in no time. Perhaps they will have disappeared even before you arrive, and then you can console yourself with other animals or birds that luck will bring your way.

The descent, marked in green ▣, is through a cleft in the rock. It looks frightening, but if you are careful it's not so difficult . . . . Continue on the path and you will find yourself at the bottom of a kind of cauldron or crater, a kind of lovely widening of the upper course of Nahal Roded. At the foot of the cliff water drips and collects in a small concrete pool, and this is the source of the name, En Netafim. The Arabs called the place En El-Katar, meaning the spring of drops. The British built a small concrete pool here in which the water collected and served the Bedouin, and also later the hikers in the region. The old pool was damaged and the one in which the water collects today was restored by the local Field School. Until not long ago the water tasted good. In how many places in Israel could one still drink water straight from the spring? Unfortunately, now this is one of the places where, although there is an abundant flow, the water has a high concentration of chlorine.

From above, look to the left of the spring. You will see a kind of "seam" in the hill. You can clearly discern the shifting of the strata, with the right side dropping and the left rising, or vice versa. But the result is definitely visible.

You can return through the same cleft you came down or take the path encircling the cauldron from the east marked in black ▣ .

▲
A view of En Netafim from above

► En Netafim: at the bottom of the cliff

Different Types of Rock at the
RED CANYON

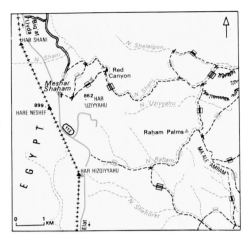

The approach is from Road 112, parallel to the Egyptian border. A little to the south of Har Shani a signpost indicates the route to Nahal Shani and the Red Canyon. A path marked in green ▭ leads to the canyon.

It's strange to think that reaching the Red Canyon is an easy matter. A paved road from Elat or from Uvda Valley, and that's it! Once it was not so simple. Here, for example, is part of the description of a touring route in the sixties: "Gay Shani (the Red Canyon) about 25 kilometers on foot . . . a difficult climb . . . we meet the car only in the evening after coming up from Nahal Raham to upper Nahal Shani and go back down towards Nahal Raham or to the Arava in one of the other riverbeds . . . ."

Later on it became possible to tour by car or by jeep. A dirt road was cut parallel to the Egyptian border. This was Yair Road (named in memory of Yair Peled, an officer and scout who was killed in 1959 in an encounter with a Bedouin near the Egyptian border). One of the difficult sections was the ascent from En Netafim to the border points, 728 and 833.

After the Six Day War the situation improved. In Biqa't HaYareach, which had been across the border, were roads that combined into one good route, leading to the foot of Mount Uziyyahu. Since then the trip to the canyon has become a simple matter for private cars and buses, and not only for good walkers, but for elementary school children as well. Literally a trip for any beginner . . . .

Later there was another setback. The Egyptian border "returned" with the peace treaties, and again the way was open only to jeeps, and those only on the dirt road that had meanwhile deteriorated. But today all this is past history. There is a new road and the Red Canyon is almost a regular station.

And yet . . . when you walk along the green-marked path ▭ in Nahal Shani you enter into a world of colored sandstones. The works of nature are fantastic. To the left and right colors and more colors.

Go a little further and you will be at the mouth of the Red Canyon — a narrow gorge cut into the dark red sandstone. Red below, multicolored sandstone above — red and white, purple and white, and a narrow crack of blue sky in some sections of the canyon. It is about 150 meters long and wide enough for people — between two and three meters. Once in a while there is a waterfall which is easily surmounted with the help of a ladder or railings that are found here, and walls rising to a height of 25-30 meters. Below, as if to make it easier for us, the area is wider. Floods widened the riverbed and created rock niches to rest in or wait for friends who are still sliding down the falls. When you "finish," the canyon the river widens and changes rock surface and color. You will enter an area of light-colored limestone. To return, climb the path from the south of the gorge and look at the Red Canyon again, this time from above.

▲
Astragalus north of the Red Canyon (April)

▶ The Red Canyon

To the "Finger of God" at
NAHAL ETEQ

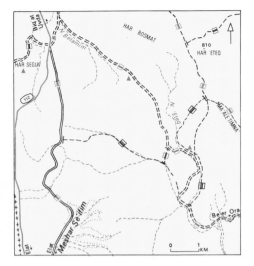

The turnoff is from Road 112, which runs parallel to the Egyptian border. The route, only for jeeps and the like, is indicated first by the red marker ▨ and then, to Nahal Betamim, by the blue marker ▨ to the canyon at Nahal Eteq.

This site is exceptional, and at present can only be reached on foot, by jeep, camel, or something similar.

First, the name. Not far from the site is a valley bearing a similar name — Biqat Sayyarim. You should know that the number of names increases in proportion to the number of trackers. It means Scouts' Valley and is named after the Palmach trackers who in the War of Independence searched for and found a way to circumvent the hills of Elat and go directly down to the shore of the Gulf of Elat. This took place during Operation Uvda, which is also the name of the valley next to Scouts' Valley.

Later, Ma'ale Sayyarim came into being during the training of a crack reconnaissance unit which first prepared a passage "only" for jeeps and command cars. Whoever passed through in its early days knows that it was a very difficult ascent. Here and there the scouts covered the ramps with metal grids in order to facilitate the ascent, and here and there they didn't look (out of fear) at the sides of the road which didn't seem wide enough for a vehicle. Here and there, too, they helped to clear away stones and to guide. Even then, different names were given to some sections: the Hava Ascent or the Hava Pass; the Nabot Pass; and other names apparently connected with the scouts and their girlfriends . . . .

When the ascent was opened it became a major route for special vehicles from the Negev hills to the Arraba around Elat. Remember that even today there are only two convenient roads that go down to the Arraba in this area. The northernmost road is the Grofit Pass which is north of Yotvata, and the new road that today runs parallel to the border (112). A few years ago part of the Pass was widened. A truck full of hikers whose driver was tempted to go down this road got stuck, and the road had to be widened in order to get them out.

Trackers' Pass goes down to Nahal Raham and from there to Be'er Ora, an area which is a closed Nature Reserve. Hikers are permitted to go down to Eteq Canyon and to "The Finger of God."

The canyon is beautiful. You can go down and walk around it. It has several waterfalls and waterholes and a touch of beauty is added by the flint "potatoes" in its walls. In its lower part the walls reach a height of 50 meters, which is certainly impressive. After rain and floods the waterholes at the bottom of the river are filled and then it is a beautiful and joyful sight.

The phenomenon that attracts many people here is the beautiful creasing of the layers in the northern wall. This creasing is formed as a result of strong pressure on layers of hard limestone which is surrounded by softer limestone. In geological language this is "rolling" but in hikers' terms it is simply "the finger of God."

▶ The Canyon at Nahal Eteq

▶
"The finger of God" — creasing of the layers at Nahal Eteq